The End of Social Inequality?

The End of
Social Inequality?

Class, Status and Power under
State Socialism

DAVID LANE
Professor of Sociology, University of Birmingham

London
GEORGE ALLEN & UNWIN
Boston   Sydney

George Allen & Unwin (Publishers) Ltd,
40 Museum Street, London WC1A 1LU, UK

George Allen & Unwin (Publishers) Ltd,
Park Lane, Hemel Hempstead, Herts HP2 4TE, UK

Allen & Unwin, Inc.,
9 Winchester Terrace, Winchester, Mass. 01890, USA

George Allen & Unwin Australia Pty Ltd,
8 Napier Street, North Sydney, NSW 2060, Australia

First published in 1982

The End of Social Inequality? Class, Status and Power under State Socialism is
the successor volume to *The End of Inequality? Stratification under State
Socialism* published by Penguin Books in 1971.

British Library Cataloguing in Publication Data

Lane, David
   The end of social inequality?
1. Social classes—Russia   2. Equality
I. Title
305'.0947   GF601

ISBN 0-04-323024-5
ISBN 0-04-323025-3 Pbk

Library of Congress Cataloging in Publication Data

Lane, David Stuart.
   The end of social inequality?
"Successor volume to The end of inequality? Stratification under state
socialism, published by Penguin Books in 1971" – T. p. verso.
Bibliography: p.
Includes index.
1. Social classes – Europe, Eastern. 2. Social classes – Soviet Union.
3. Communism and society.
I. Title.
HN380.Z9S645   305.5'0947   82-4101
ISBN 0-04-323024-5   AACR2
ISBN 0-04-323025-3 (pbk.)

Set in 11 on 12 point Plantin by Typesetters (Birmingham) Ltd,
and printed in Great Britain
by Billing and Sons Ltd, Guildford, London and Worcester.

Contents

Foreword

Classes and status groups are, in Weber's phrase, 'phenomena of the distribution of power in a community'. But they are also manifestations of what Durkheim called a society's 'moral classification of men and things', which is ultimately a 'religious' phenomenon. The study of stratification, then, involves an understanding of society as a totality: its economy polity and its system of values and beliefs. Each form of stratification has a legal basis (even when this is one of formal equality of citizenship); it has its own 'political economy'; its own ideological rationale. These conditions determine the extent of class antagonisms and the degree of solidification of status structures; and such variations in the shape of stratification from one society to another constitute the main subject-matter of this branch of sociology. Underlying these variations, however, basically similar forces are at work. Societies are systems distinguished by their peculiar need for solidarity and their occasional liability to schism. And because social stratification is uniquely expressive of these fundamental alternations of consensus and disorder in society as a whole, it is the object of sociological study *par excellence*. Unequal and never wholly stable distributions of goods and power are the source of an ever-present potential for conflict the actualisation of which is contrary to the nature of a status hierarchy which seeks to legitimise privilege and disadvantage and to generate wants in accordance with its own moral matrix. This regulation is always imperfect, partly because the accumulation and dissolution of power has a momentum which is inconsiderate of established expectancies of status. Newly created power has a hunger for legitimation in a status order that is congruent with its own structure just as status, once formed, endeavours to appropriate nascent power which might threaten its authorisation of inequality. But the regulation is also imperfect because the logic of status reaches beyond the world of inequality as it finds it and to which it must accommodate. Its horizons are ideal, and the tension between ideology and reality is an additional reason why adherence to a status order is never unconditional, even on the part of those who are most indulged by its dispensation. Indeed, the tendency of status hierarchies to call forth their own negation in the ideal of equality is very widespread. In many cases, the influence of this ideal has been only very feeble, peripheral and intermittent; but in some it has become the central activating principle of massive social change – thereby adding the 'sociology of classlessness' to the agenda of the study of stratification.

David Lane's book addresses itself directly to this latter problem by posing the question: Has inequality been abolished in state-socialist societies? His answer provides an interpretation of a diversity of factual material relating to the social structure of the Soviet Union (as well as other societies in Eastern Europe following its political model) and, at the same time, of the unusually explicit theory which that society has about itself. Dr Lane conveys his specialist knowledge of the subject in a style which will make his work accessible to a wider audience than just students of sociology.

DAVID LOCKWOOD

Preface

In this expanded and revised version, I have updated the statistics, revised the bibliography, rewritten and rearranged much of the material which appeared in *The End of Inequality?* in 1971. I have also added many new sections to incorporate the results of new research which has been published since that date.

Acknowledgement is made to the following for permission to use copyright material: University of Chicago Press; Polish Scientific Publishers; Pall Mall Press; Professor Bogdan Denitch (for 'International study of opinion makers'); Dr S. Bialer; Central Statistical Office, Warsaw; Central Statistical Office, Budapest; Professor David Lockwood; Columbia University Press.

Throughout the book words have been anglicised to the extent of omitting all diacritical signs.

Introduction

From time immemorial radicals have opposed inequality. Thinkers have advocated the redistribution of wealth from the rich to the poor, of power from the rulers to the exploited. Radical men of action have sought to change society from a state of what they see as degradation to one where any man's rights, possessions, power and honour are equal to the next man's. But to abolish or reduce such inequality requires more than moral platitudes. Why do men inherit a world of inequality, what are its causes, how does one abolish them? The politician and sociologist make different assumptions about the causes of inequality. The former is constrained in his appraisal by his political interests and by those of his supporters, whereas the sociologist, who may also often be committed to social change, attempts to formulate his analysis in more general terms by establishing laws about social structures and their transformation. The experience of the Soviet Union is particularly relevant to these problems, because in October 1917 the Bolsheviks attempted to lay the foundation-stones for a society in which men would live in harmony and equality. The October Revolution was not concerned with the amelioration of conditions in Tsarist Russia from the viewpoint of liberal ideas of distributive justice, but with changing the fundamental structure of power and authority. How far have the Communists succeeded in their quest? Have they found that immutable social laws have turned to stone their good intentions? Were the Marxist theories which the Russian Bolsheviks used to justify their action false, or were they betrayed by men whose political interests debased these ideals? It is hoped that this study of social stratification of state-socialist society may provide some of the answers to these questions.

'State socialist' is a label used to describe societies, modelled on the Soviet Union, which are distinguished by a state-owned, a more or less centrally controlled, planned economy and by a politically dominant Communist Party. At the same time, the cultural and social orders of such states exhibit considerable variation and it has been found impossible to cover their diversity in a short book. The Soviet Union, of course, occupies a dominant political position in Eastern Europe and it is also sociologically interesting because the Communists have been in power there for much longer than in other countries. Therefore it has been taken as the main subject of study except when discussing some topics where the paucity of source materials on the Soviet Union has made it necessary to refer to research carried out in other Eastern European countries. I have tried to give a balanced picture of both Western and 'indigenous' research.

While it could once be said that empirical research in state-socialist societies was conceptually and methodologically inadequate to say very much about the system of class and strati-fication, there is now a considerable amount of data available and many conclusions may be made with confidence. While we may be fairly sure of the distribution and size of various types of inequalities – or 'outputs' of the socio-political system – the explanation of why such privileges and advantages persist under state socialism becomes of primary concern to sociologists.

In a short book of this kind it is impossible to give a full descriptive account of the many facets of social stratification in Soviet society. I have tried to interweave theoretical, historical and contemporary aspects of Soviet society to show how Marxist ideology has influenced the official description of Soviet reality and to show how Marx's views of class have been adapted to describe the dictatorship of the proletariat and the Soviet notion of a socialist society. The most important issue here is the relevance of Marx's notion of class to the actual structure of power after the Bolshevik Revolution. In Chapter 1 are described the original views of Marx and their adaptation by Soviet Communists in the description of Russia before and after the Revolution. This involves a brief historical review of Soviet developments between 1917 and 1956: a contrast between the class structure of Tsarist Russia and the dictatorship of the proletariat (between 1917 and 1936) and an examination of the first stage of Soviet socialism (1936 to 1956). In Chapters 2 to 4 empirical research on social stratification in mainly post-1956 Soviet (and East European) society is summarised. Much of this work considers status and hierarchy rather than class in a

Marxist sense. These chapters also review the literature which has sought to make comparisons between the structure of Eastern European societies and Western capitalist ones, as well as other studies of social hierarchy and political inequality in state-socialist society. However, not wishing to restrict the study to a *Soviet* Marxist framework, I have outlined other approaches to Soviet society. In Chapter 5 several different models of the Soviet social order are discussed. Here are considered some of the more traditional Marxist critiques stemming from Trotsky's orientation, others, including those within state-socialist societies, who emphasise conflictual relationships and finally liberal-democratic theorists who depict a totalitarian or bureaucratic type of society. The earlier chapters have as their subject more the distributional aspects of stratification, while the later ones are concerned with relations between people. Finally, in the conclusion, some generalisations about stratification stemming from the experience of state-socialist society are put forward.

The arrangement of the book facilitates the discussion of three interrelated problems of social stratification as they apply to state-socialist societies. First, there is the relevance of the Marxist notion of *class*, by which we mean a social and economic group at its roots differentiated by its 'relationship to the means of production' with a common political interest against other classes. Class in this sense is a tool in the analysis of history, a causal factor in the transformation of societies. The important question here is the nature of the political structure of a society in which classes, in the formal Marxist sense, have been abolished. This is the subject-matter of Chapters 1 and 5. Secondly, we are concerned with the nature of *social inequality* in a state-socialist society. Social inequality refers to the uneven distribution of goods and values among the population in the sense that one group may have more income or education than another; and this aspect of stratification is the concern of Chapter 2. Closely connected to inequality is the *ranking* and *privilege* of individuals or groups on a scale of superiority or inferiority; and these are the topics of Chapter 3. In Chapter 4 we examine the related question of the extent to which individual statuses are available to open recruitment or conversely are restricted to certain groups.

1 The Impact of Marxist Ideas in Russia before and after the October Revolution

MARXISM AND THE PRE-REVOLUTIONARY BACKGROUND

The first aspect of stratification mentioned above was that of class and the main task of this chapter is to explain what role class played in Marx's theory, how his ideas were developed by his followers in Tsarist Russia and how later they were adapted to the structure of the Soviet Union.

In the original theory of Marx, class occupied the centre of the stage as the prime mover of historical development. Classes were social entities formed on the basis of economic relations. Ownership relations were the prime, though not exclusive, determinants of class position.

> What makes wage labourers, capitalists and landlords constitute the three great classes?
> At first glance – the identity of revenues and sources of revenue. There are three great social groups whose members, the individuals forming them, live on wages, profit and ground rent respectively, on the realisation of their labour power, their capital and their landed property. (Marx, 1867, pp. 862–3)

The relationship to the means of production, or market relations, was the basis on which classes, the chief agents of history, were formed. Marx was less concerned with the other two elements of social stratification mentioned above, inequality and ranking. To be sure, they are related: the ruling class, by virtue of its economic power, has in the eyes of many, high prestige or honour; and the exploited have what might be called a low and congruent ranking in terms of power, income and status. Soviet Marxists have tended to concentrate attention on the element of property relations inherent in Marxist thought and have applied this rather mechanically to power relations and social stratification.

Many contemporary Marxists, in attempting to grapple with the complexities of modern capitalism, have pointed to other aspects of class position and have emphasised the role of authority, of rights over other men (domination) which may arise from political power widely conceived. (See discussion in Parkin, 1979.) These criteria become a major foundation, as we shall see below (pp. 140–6), in the orientation of many critical Marxist approaches to state socialism.

Marx concentrated on explaining the inner logic of social change and emphasised that social transformations could not take place independently of the economic structure. But ownership relations are only one part of the economic basis, the other being the forces of production, that is the character of technology or the kind of tools (including intellectual ones) which are utilised at a certain stage of development. Marx describes the relationship of social transformation to economic structure and the conditions of social transformation in two well-known passages. He says:

> No social order ever perishes before all the productive forces for which there is room in it have developed; and new, higher relations of production never appear before the material conditions for their existence have matured in the womb of the old society itself. (1958*b*, p. 363)

He also wrote:

> Men make their own history, but they do not make it just as they please; they do not make it under circumstances chosen by themselves, but under circumstances directly encountered, given and transmitted from the past. (1958*a*, p. 247)

While the conflict of economic classes dominates history, the characteristics of the dominant and exploited classes will depend on the technological level of development of the society. Marx defined five 'ideal type' societies: Asiatic (or primitive communism), ancient, feudal, bourgeois and communist (1958*b*, Vol. 1, p. 363). These may be regarded as the main forms of civilisation: ancient society was characterised by the ownership of slaves, feudal society had a ruling class which possessed land, in bourgeois society the capitalist class owned the large-scale enterprises producing economic wealth and in communist society no classes would exist.

It is perhaps worth stressing that here the dominant class under capitalism is interpreted in the sense of a social group's power being based on the extraction of surplus value, derived from the working class through the process of the market, from the ownership of the proceeds of capital. It is a much wider concept than that of a political class – those who occupy positions in the state – which carries out the function of ruling; though, of course, under capitalism this stratum is a crucial part of the dominant class. Social transformations are limited by the level of technological advance and political action must be related to the development of the productive forces. If we interpret Marx literally, a communist society without social classes would necessarily follow the capitalist form, for only after this stage would the technology be able to sustain economic abundance. Let us now consider how well Russia fitted into his scheme.

In the late nineteenth and early twentieth centuries, the Russian Empire did not fit conveniently into any one of Marx's ideal types. It could be said to contain elements of feudal and bourgeois societies. It was feudal in the sense that the chief form of production was a manorial type of agriculture on which rested the dominant landowning class, the basis of Tsarist power. But, in addition, industrial capitalism was making great strides: a railway system and other communications and large-scale industrial complexes were set up in many parts of Russia. (Industrial production increased five-fold between 1885 and 1913. See comparative figures in Gerschenkron, 1947, p. 156.) Peculiar features of this economic development were, on the one hand, the absence of a dynamic indigenous bourgeoisie in the sense of private owners of the means of production and, on the other, the presence of an urban proletariat. The Russian bourgeoisie was small and ineffective and industrial development had been sponsored by the Russian government. In the late nineteenth century much industry was either formally government-owned and controlled, or foreign-owned and subsidised by the state. The proletariat – factory and mining workers – numbered some 2½ million in 1913 out of a total population of 139 million. Those drawing a wage or salary from any source accounted for 16·7 per cent of the population, and another 7·2 per cent were handicraftsmen employed on their own account. Though the industrial proletariat was small, industrial enterprises were large: whereas 53 per cent of Russian workers were employed in factories with 500 or more men, in the USA at the same time (1910) only 33 per cent were so employed.

The crucial characteristics of Russian society, then, were that the capitalist mode of production was present only in embryo form and the indigenous capitalist class was weak. In so far as the latter did exist, it was protected by the 'feudal' powers. The proletariat, which was recruited from the oppressed peasantry, was being organised in Marxist parties which had a greater influence in the nascent working class in Russia than in the more slowly developing Western European societies. One of the reasons for this was that almost any kind of political association was banned in Russia. 'Gradualist' political parties and trade unions did not develop to the same extent as in other capitalist countries and in their absence it was not possible for the working class to be 'incorporated' into the regime. Increasingly, they turned instead to the leadership of illegal Marxist revolutionary groups.

Marxist analysis of the revolutionary process considers not only the consciousness of the ascendant class, but also points to the weakening of the social support for the dominant one. In the typical transition from feudalism to capitalism, important strata among the cultural intelligentsia (particularly among the clergy), the army and among the aristocracy, throw in their lot with the rising commercial and industrial classes. In Russia, the absence of such an indigenous class left many of the strata thrown up by industrialisation or made marginal by the poverty of the aristocracy without a clear class location and many of the intellectuals became identified (out of turn, as it were) with the urban proletariat and became advocates of Marxist social democracy.

Faced with this situation, 'classical' and 'radical' Marxists came to fundamentally different conclusions about the course of social change in Russia. The 'classical' school, epitomised by the Mensheviks, thought that the proletariat could play a small part in bringing about a *bourgeois* revolution. Until this had been achieved and until the bourgeoisie had transformed feudal Russia into a modern industrial state, all talk of socialism or of the 'dictatorship of the proletariat' was premature and inimical to the interests of the working class. The workers, they argued, should form as wide a trade-union type of party as conditions would allow. The 'radicals' (Lenin and the Bolsheviks) regarded this view either as 'revisionist' or as a formalist interpretation of Marx. In Russian conditions, they said, the traditional form of social democratic party was impractical. A select party of Marxists, led by professional revolutionaries, was apposite to Russian conditions. In Russia, they believed, a socialist revolution was possible. They argued that capitalism should be analysed as a world economic system, which the First World War brought to explosion point. In 1917 only a spark was needed. That spark could be kindled in the country where capitalism was weakest and proletarian organisation strongest – in Russia. The proletariat, therefore, should not passively wait for the full development of a bourgeois society, for it was doubtful if the Russian bourgeoisie had sufficient class-consciousness to fulfil its historic role. The correct course for the Russian working class from this point of view was to abolish the autocratic system and seize political power, then, after completing their own revolution, the victorious proletariat in the advanced countries would help secure a communist system in Russia. (On Lenin's theory of revolution, see D. Lane, 1981.)

These ideas help one to understand the nature of social and political change in Soviet Russia after the Bolshevik seizure of power in October 1917. The uprising of the advanced Western proletariat did not materialise and the Soviet government found itself ruling in one of the economically most underdeveloped and backward countries in Europe. In a Marxist sense, *politically* the ruling class was now the proletariat, but the society over which it ruled was not socialist: it could not strictly speaking be *de facto* a socialist society because the economic forces had not outgrown the technological level of the capitalist stage of production. After seizing political power, Lenin and the Russian Communist Party consciously set out to complete two tasks involving the transformation of the society inherited after the revolution. (The name, Russian Communist Party – Bolsheviks – was adopted in 1918; before this time the Bolsheviks operated as a faction of the Russian Social Democratic Labour Party. In 1952 the name of the party was changed to Communist Party of the Soviet Union.) These were, first, the destruction of the system of social classes inherited from Tsarist Russia, and secondly, the creation of a system of social relations embodying the new socialist order.

Soviet Marxists have distinguished four distinct historical phases in the development of Soviet society:

(1) October 1917 to 1925: a period of social revolution.
(2) 1926 to 1936: years of socialist industrialisation.
(3) 1936 to 1956: the epoch in which the first phase of building socialism was completed.
(4) 1956 to the present: the second phase of socialist construction, the building of communist society. (*Marksistsko-leninskaya filosofiya i sotsiologiya v SSSR i Evropeiskikh sotsialisticheskikh stran*, 1965, pp. 8–9)

In the 1970s and early 1980s, Soviet theorists refer to their own society as one of 'developed socialism'. This concept was first used by Brezhnev in 1970 in a speech commemorating the hundredth anniversary of Lenin's birth. (See Evans, 1977, p. 412.) It should be noted that none of these phases is 'communist': communism as a Marxist stage of society requires both a higher level of productive forces and of class-consciousness. The term 'communist' is used by the government and Party of the USSR to distinguish its goals and aspirations from those of Western social democratic parties and states.

In Marxist-Leninist terms, these four historical stages may be combined into two analytically distinct societies: the phase of the dictatorship of the proletariat (1917 to 1936); and the building of socialist society (1936 to the present). The chief theoretical distinction between these societies from the Soviet Marxist viewpoint lies in the character of class relations, for while the dictatorship of the proletariat still entailed *class* conflict, socialist society did not.

THE 'DICTATORSHIP OF THE PROLETARIAT'

Period of Social Revolution

In Leninist theory, the downfall of the Tsarist Empire ushered in neither 'socialism' nor 'communism'. The immediate task of the Bolsheviks was to ensure the rule of the proletariat: rather than being democratic, the political structure was defined officially as the 'dictatorship of the proletariat'. This was justified on the ground that the working class had to defend itself against a possible counter-revolution. The social structure of the 'dictatorship of the proletariat' involved a polarisation of classes: on one side was the proletariat in a 'friendly alliance' (*smychka*) with the peasantry, on the other was the increasingly dispossessed bourgeoisie and aristocracy.

This world view shaped the Bolsheviks' immediate social policy. The changes which followed the seizure of political power by the Bolsheviks were introduced gradually, rather than at one fell swoop. Within a year after the Revolution of 1917, decrees had been passed nationalising the land and the key industries – coal, oil, iron, steel, chemicals and textiles. By December 1920 nationalisation was extended to all enterprises employing more than five workers using any kind of mechanical power or to those employing more than ten without mechanical power. These measures, coupled with laws restricting inheritance, were an attack on the landlords and capitalists. The dispossession of the ownership-based classes was paralleled by the loss of position and privileges of other previously dominant groups. All titles and ranks were abolished. Many senior state bureaucrats were dismissed; church and state were separated. The members of the previous ruling classes lost their civic rights; they could not vote or join the Communist Party. There was a period of intense class struggle: the large estates were seized and split up among independent peasant proprietors. Members of the technical and administrative strata, whose previous class position identified them with the possessing classes, were 'declassed' and made to work, as it were, for the proletariat. They lost their privileges, their salaries were significantly reduced, often their houses were shared with the poor, and during the periods of food rationing they received 'according to their work', which in practice often meant the lowest grade of ration card (Lenin, 1965, pp. 107–17). These socially levelling or 'egalitarian' policies were seen as meeting the demands of the class struggle. They were essentially *class* changes.

But side by side with such attacks on the old order, other more positive measures were introduced by the Bolsheviks and these also affected social stratification and inequality. Wages were equalised (see p. 21) and other measures removed various forms of discrimination and advantage which were prevalent before the Revolution. Women were given equal legal rights with men. Campaigns were conducted to make the population literate. Polytechnic education, involving all children in manual and mental work, was advocated as a means of reducing the social distance between the various kinds of labour. The educational system, dedicated to the development of a new communist man, was organised on child-centred, non-authoritarian principles.

In addition to such 'planned' equalitarianism, the early years of the Revolution were ones of turmoil, and although the Communist Party was ostensibly the vanguard of the proletariat, it was not always in control. In this situation the workers 'introduced communism' by instituting workers' control and the situation was seen by some as the beginning of an era of free goods. It need hardly be added that the latter had nothing to do with the social theory of the Bolsheviks but was a result of the chaos of revolution and civil war. 'Workers' control' was indeed the official Bolshevik policy for a time, but it did not sanctify workers' power in the factories independently of the central authorities or of the Communist Party, rather it entailed – as the leaders saw it – the exercise of a check over the bourgeoisie and management, in the interests of the new state of workers and peasants.

Yet despite the measures directed against it, the bourgeoisie as a class was not completely obliterated. After the period of Civil War (1917–22), small factories, retail trade and almost the whole of agricultural production remained under private management and produced surplus for profit. The Bolshevik government's edict nationalising the land had occurred concurrently with the small proprietory peasantry seizing and splitting up the large estates. Consequently, they worked the land in the form of private plots and traded their surplus with the towns. Thus, until the collectivisation of agriculture in 1929, a large area of private enterprise and bourgeois values prevailed and in the countryside the Bolsheviks had not yet a wide social basis of political support.

The Bolsheviks' social legislation was also directed against other important institutions of the old social structure. The Russian patriarchal family was held to embody bourgeois values and to be an element conserving the old regime. The government's early decrees were therefore designed to undermine this institution. The fact of cohabitation and a common household became recognised as marriage. Divorce was easily obtainable by either spouse and the legal status of husband and wife was made equal before the courts. Children born outside registered marriage were given the same rights with regard to their parents as children born of it. In general, Soviet family legislation in this period succeeded in weakening parental authority.

Even during the immediate post-revolutionary period, it is noteworthy that many features of the old regime were retained. Industrial discipline was based on a hierarchical management pattern and syndicalism and workers' management of production were repudiated. The monogamous family, albeit in a weakened form, was preserved and sexual licence was deplored. It must be made clear that it was *not* the intention of the Bolsheviks to abolish the wage system or to introduce the equal distribution of commodities as advocated by Anarchists (Kropotkin, 1888). We shall see later that high wage differentials also characterised Soviet Russia under a later phase of the 'dictatorship of the proletariat'.

The relatively underdeveloped state of the country and the

Bolsheviks' expectation that the intervention of the advanced West European proletariat was imminent are reasons why 'socialism' was not immediately introduced. In this initial period, the 'dictatorship of the proletariat' was regarded as a transitionary and temporary one.

By the mid-1920s, however, the Soviet leaders came to accept that the Western proletariat would not complete a successful revolution against the bourgeoisie, and the Russian Communists turned, therefore, to create a socio-economic base which would secure their rule. The original justification of the Revolution in October 1917 was that it was the first step towards the establishment of, in Lenin's words, 'a socialist organisation of society and the victory of socialism in all countries'. But in 1926 Stalin argued that the first stage of communism, the 'socialist' stage, could be completed in Russia 'without the preliminary victory of the proletarian revolution in other countries'. Social change of a more radical kind was envisaged in the USSR after Stalin's statement: it included the obliteration of what were regarded as the remaining bourgeois strata, the smallholding peasantry, and the creation of a large working class and 'communist' intelligentsia. This was the second phase of the 'dictatorship of the proletariat'. Some opponents of Stalin and the Party leadership, notably Trotsky, put the emphasis more on the international context, on the importance of revolution in the advanced countries of the West and stressed the impossibility of achieving socialism in the backward conditions of Russia and the hostile world environment.

Industrialisation and Collectivisation

The expropriation of the large capitalist magnates and landed gentry in the early years of the Revolution had been carried out relatively easily, for it had widespread popular support and these strata made up a small proportion of the population. The problem of the smallholding peasantry was quite a different matter, for in 1928 there were some 25 million individual peasant farms. Moreover, the October Revolution had been carried out, according to official Leninist theory, by an alliance between the proletariat and the peasantry which was founded on the hostility of both these groups to the autocracy, big land-owners and the magnates of capital. But the individual plot-farming peasant did not have a proletarian socialist ideology. The peasant's mentality was conditioned by tradition. He sought to realise his long-held aspirations for individual proprietory rights and wanted to preserve his firm attachment to the soil. After 1917 and the seizure of the land, the class interests of the peasantry, in so far as it sought private production for profit, were inimical to the ruling Communist Party. Had the Russian revolution spread to the West, governments representing the European proletariat might have supported the Russian Communists with economic aid and the 'peasant problem' might have been slowly resolved. But the Russian Communists had to deal with the problem alone. They did so by a policy of collectivisation which involved the expropriation of most of the peasant smallholdings and the creation of *kolkhozy*, or collective farms, which brought the land under the administrative control of the Bolshevik government. One of the most momentous changes in modern times involved the transfer of peasant plots, stock and seeds to collective farms. When the collectivisation drive began in 1929, only 3·9 per cent of households had been collectivised, but by 1938 93·5 per cent of them were so organised. Behind these figures lies a story of the seizure of peasant property and of the extermination, or transportation to Siberia, of an estimated 5 million peasants.

The second strand in Stalin's policy of building a socialist society in Soviet Russia was rapid industrialisation which was carried out in the first two Five-Year Plans (1928–32; 1933–7). Except to note that the Soviet average annual rate of growth of all industry between 1928 and 1932 has been estimated at 20·35 per cent (Gerschenkron, 1947, p. 161), the details of this economic development need not detain us here. Rapid industrial-isation did involve, however, a dramatic change in the occupational structure. Between 1928 and 1937 the number of manual and non-manual workers employed in industry rose from 3·8 to 10·1 million – a two-and-a-half-fold increase. In heavy industry, the number of manual workers more than doubled between 1929 and 1936, rising from 2·8 million to 6·2 million (Rashin, 1961, pp. 16, 29). Similarly, the urban population rose from 19 per cent of the total in 1929 to 33 per cent in 1940.

The official Soviet figures which summarise the main changes are shown on Table 1.1. Whereas in 1913 only 17 per cent of the population was dependent on wage labour (manual and non-manual employment), by 1939 manual and non-manual workers accounted for about half of the population, the number of self-employed peasants and craftsmen had dwindled from 67 per cent to some 3 per cent and capitalists, at least in a formal sense, no longer existed. It is worth pointing out that occupational change in England and Wales has followed a similar trend. In the nineteenth century the main shift from the country to the town occurred: between 1911 and 1951 the numbers of employers and self-employed drastically declined, those of the professions and skilled labour rose (Hobsbawm, 1968, diagrams 8–12). What then were the political relations which lay behind these figures?

Table 1.1 *Social Structure of Soviet Population 1913, 1928, 1939 (Official Figures)*

	1913	1928	1939
Manual and non-manual workers	17	17	50
Collective-farm peasantry and craftsmen	0	3	47
Independent peasants and craftsmen	67	75	3
Bourgeoisie, landowners, merchants, *kulaks* (rich independent peasants)	16	5	0
TOTAL (including non-working members of families)	100	100	100

Source: Tsentral'noe (1966, p. 42). In absolute terms the number of employed manual and non-manual workers rose from 11·4 million in 1913 to 62 million in 1960 and by 1980 they totalled 112·5 million. The number of employed non-manuals increased from 2·9 million in 1926 to 20·5 million in 1959 and 33·6 million in 1980.

After the October Revolution, the working class was, in theory, the dominant class sustaining the dictatorship of the proletariat. This concept gives rise to a number of political and social problems at various levels of power. A dominant class may be defined in an abstract manner, in terms of the class which has legal ownership of the means of production, distribution and exchange. To carry out the functions of domination it must secure enforcement through the state. But a dominant class cannot rule by controlling or occupying only the élite positions, it must ensure also that many other posts of authority are filled by politically reliable men. In an industrial society such positions require training in specific skills and techniques. The Bolsheviks recognised that *to administer* the state specialist knowledge and experience were necessary: political commitment was no substitute for knowledge. Here the Bolsheviks were in a dilemma for many of the technical specialists inherited from Tsarist Russia were either of bourgeois social extraction or regarded themselves as bourgeois, and such men, it was thought, could not be trusted to work conscientiously for the new rulers. On the other hand, the main supporters of the Communist Party – the urban proletariat – had neither the education nor the skill necessary to man the command posts of the society.

The Communist government solved this problem in two ways: first, by political sanctions and a policy of political placement; and secondly, by a crash programme of education. Political sanctions involved the use of terror as a mechanism to ensure conformity to the will of the political leadership. This was directed against those strata who were thought to be sympathetic to the dispossessed classes. As early as July 1918 Lenin had said that Soviet power had to be guaranteed 'by putting the bourgeoisie under suspicion and carrying out mass terror against it' (see Carr, 1950, p. 167). Carr sums up Bolshevik policy as follows: 'The essence of the terror was its class character. It selected its victims on the ground, not of specific offences, but of their membership of the possessing classes' (p. 168). The fear of arrest, imprisonment or death was used not only to deter a counter-revolutionary rising, but to make the population adaptable and amenable to the Communist political leadership. In addition to these measures, political commissars were appointed to the Red Army with power to countermand orders. Even though the technical control of industrial enterprises had to be left in the hands of the pre-revolutionary bourgeois specialists, 'Red Directors' were appointed to supervise their activity and to ensure that they did not sabotage the Communist political order (Bienstock, Schwarz and Yugow, 1948, ch. 1; in 1925 only 1·3 per cent of technical factory chiefs were Communists, Drobizhev, 1961, p. 64). At higher levels of economic administration, the authorities had succeeded as early as 1927 in promoting sufficient Communist Party members to guarantee control of the industrial trusts. By that year, 65 per cent of their members at director level and 98 per cent of the chairmen were Party members (Drobizhev, 1961, p. 63).

From Insurgent to Ruling Party

During this process the Communist Party underwent a transformation. From being a secret underground party of revolutionaries, it now became a ruling body. Its members experienced upward social mobility. We may appreciate the magnitude of this change by examining the composition of the Party before and after the Revolution. There can be no doubt that the leaders of the Bolshevik Party before the Revolution were from the educated middle social strata. Of the fifty-one delegates at the Party's founding congress in 1903 only three had been workers, though later (1907) their number rose to over half of the 218 delegates. At the lower levels of the Party, the Bolshevik activists were largely recruited from the working class (D. Lane, 1969). The social origins of the leaders may be clearly seen by studying Table 1.2, which shows the membership of the Party's Central Committee. These were the men who later experienced rapid upward mobility from lower-middle status groups to the apex of the power structure after 1917. It is pertinent to note the very small number of workers in the Party élite, and the figures cited include not one peasant. At the lower levels of the Party, workers predominated: in 1905 and in 1917, they constituted some 60 per

Table 1.2 *Social Origin of Bolshevik Party Élite, 1903–18*

Party congress	*Social origin of Central Committee as percentage*	
	Manual workers	*Non-manual*
II 1903	0	100
III 1905	0	100
IV 1906	0	100
V 1907	6[a]	88[a]
VI 1917	12	88
VII 1918	21·7	78·3

[a] Excludes 1 of unknown social position.
Source: Bubnov (1930, cols 539–40).

cent of the total membership, but peasants made up only from 5 to 8 per cent (Bubnov, 1930, col. 533).

After 1917 Party membership grew. It rose from 115,000 on 1 January 1918 to 251,000 on 1 January 1919, and by March 1920, the Party was 611,978 strong (Bubnov, 1930, col. 53). The majority of the new members were young; at the end of 1919 over half of the Party's membership was aged under 30. It was recruited from the previous underprivileged: 5 per cent had had higher education and 8 per cent secondary; 52 per cent had been employed as manual workers; 15 per cent as peasants; and 18 per cent as non-manual workers. (Figures cited by Schapiro, 1960, pp. 233–4. For other statistics on the social composition of the Party see Semenov, 1964, p. 257.) These men provided the backbone of the new Soviet economic, administrative and political élites. By 1921, of 15,000 leading Party officials, a third were of proletarian origin, the bulk of the others originated mainly from the lower-middle status groups (Schapiro, 1960, p. 237). Large numbers of men joined the Party: membership rose from 350,000 in March 1919 to 3½ million in 1935 (Rigby, 1968, p. 52). From 1924 to 1932 the 'Lenin enrolment' attempted to give the Party a fundamentally working-class complexion. Between 1922 and 1932, the proportion of those of manual-worker origin in the Party increased from 44 per cent to 55 per cent and the share of men of non-manual-worker origin fell from 29 per cent to 8 per cent. But when one considers the actual occupations of Party members, one sees that in 1932 some 38 per cent of the total membership was in non-manual work (Rigby, 1968, p. 116). This entailed considerable upward mobility by placement through the political system and involved the adoption of ascriptive criteria for social mobility.

The second means by which the Communist government prepared the working class for positions of authority was through special provision for the improvement of the educational standards of workers. 'Workers' faculties' were formed, usually attached to existing higher educational institutions: by 1921 there were fifty-nine faculties with 25,436 students (Katuntseva, 1966, p. 17). It has been estimated that between October 1917 and 1932 between 800,000 and 900,000 men were trained for the new 'Soviet intelligentsia' (Andreyuk, 1966, p. 38). In the sphere of admission to higher education, priority was given to children of proletarian and peasant social origins. Whereas this group constituted 49·3 per cent of the intake to higher educational institutions in 1928, by 1931 the number had shot up to 65·6 per cent: in industrial institutes the respective figures were 52·9 per cent and 73·1 per cent (Drobizhev, 1961, p. 70).

Despite these changes and the clear intentions of the Communist élites to change the social composition of institutes of higher learning to the detriment of the middle-status groups and to the advantage of the workers and peasants, the 'class chances' of access to higher education were still very much in favour of the middle strata. Feldmesser has calculated that in the 1930s, as a whole, 17·5 per cent of the Soviet population was non-manual, but 42·2 per cent of college students came from this group; manual workers were only slightly over-represented with 33·9 per cent of the students and 32·3 per cent of the total population; peasants, on the other hand, constituted 46·4 per cent of the population but only 21·7 per cent of the student body (1957, p. 94). Again De Witt has estimated that at the height of the 'proletarianisation drive', 45 per cent of students in higher educational institutions were from the intelligentsia, which accounted for only 7 to 10 per cent of the total population (1961, p. 351). A detailed study of the student body in higher education in Soviet Russia between 1917 and 1928 (D. Lane, 1973) shows that there was a social gradation of educational institutions. Placement of workers from special courses was more successful in institutions related to production than in others. Aspirations, and levels of competence, for artistic and medical faculties were particularly low.

These figures are in keeping with measures of occupational mobility for the interwar period worked out on the basis of a survey of Russian *émigrés* by Miller (1960). On a comparative basis, Soviet working-class children (together with French) had the highest rate of *upward* social mobility, that is, the sons of manual working-class fathers taking up non-manual occupations. The amount of *downward* social mobility was also found, in this sample, to be very low: non-manual into manual was 15 per cent, compared to 42·1 per cent in Great Britain. The amount of movement into the 'élite' occupational strata was the highest of

19

all the countries compared: 14·5 per cent in the USSR sample, compared to only 7·8 per cent in the USA. Despite this considerable upward mobility on the part of working-class sons, Miller's comparative study shows that the advantages to Soviet middle-class sons (to improve or maintain status) were very similar to those in other countries (Denmark, France, Great Britain, Sweden and the USA) (Miller, 1960, p. 36).

We are now in a position to make a number of general points about stratification based on the history of Soviet Russia during her formative years. First, we must reject decisively the view of Bendix and Lipset that the implications for social mobility of the introduction of a new social system are not very important (1959, p. 282). The political apparatus in the first twenty years of Soviet power had a profound effect on the system of social stratification: it was responsible for the abolition of some social strata (the autocracy, the private rich peasantry); it instigated the recruitment of the previously deprived to positions of power and it was instrumental in advancing their occupational, educational and social standing. Secondly, the industrialisation process, itself a consequence of political revolution, required the recruitment of the most educable strata of the population. This entailed a modification of the Bolsheviks' policy of ascription and 'proletarianisation'. Thirdly, the change of Party role from that of an underground revolutionary body to that of a governing one, had the effect of promoting men from subordinate social positions to ruling ones.

At this point we may turn from the issue of political power and political relations to consider the extent of economic and distributive inqualities in the new Soviet order and to see in what ways, if any, the Communists reshaped the pattern of distribution.

Distribution of Rewards

Even in the early days of the Revolution, wage differentials between skilled and unskilled were recognised as necessary:

> While aspiring to equality of remuneration for all kinds of labour and to total communism, the Soviet Government

cannot consider as its task the immediate realisation of this equality at the present moment when only the first steps are being made towards the transition from capitalism to communism. (Baykov, 1947, p. 43)

Nevertheless, wage differentials were greatly reduced: in 1919, the *official* wage ratio between the highest and lowest grades of manual worker was 1¾:1 (Bergson, 1944, p. 182). But these policies were made irrelevant by the facts of the situation. In the immediate post-revolutionary period, money completely lost its value with the result that wage payments in kind were introduced. Labour was compulsorily mobilised; reward was defined in terms of social obligation: 'He who does not work, neither shall he eat'. Ration books of several categories were introduced and related to labour performed (Bergson, 1944), and the real-income differential between skilled and unskilled and between manual and non-manual labour narrowed. In the early months of 1917 earnings of the most skilled workers were 232 per cent of the unskilled labourers, whereas by 1921 they had fallen to 102 per cent. At this latter date wages in kind came to some 94 per cent of total income, and those in money only to about 6 per cent. (Figures calculated by Strumilin, cited by Baykov, 1947, p. 43.) This period (1919–21) was one of egalitarianism.

But the Communists had to face up to the problem posed by the division of labour – should workers in short supply, with higher skills and qualifications receive more of the economic surplus than their fellow workers? The short-term answer the Communists adopted was that differentials were necessary, but that they should be as small as possible. The immediate post-revolutionary period was one of emergency, geared to the need to maintain the Communists in power and to distribute resources to keep people alive, and no new practical principles of wages and labour were introduced.

With the abolition of payment in kind in 1921, wages in practice were fixed through the market – by bargaining between workers and employers. The revival of market relations generally, therefore, led to prices and wages being determined by the forces of supply and demand in much the same fashion as in pre-revolutionary Russia. (The Soviet economist Kostin cites figures which show that wage rates in pre-revolutionary Russia were similar to those of Russia in 1925–6; 1960, p. 16.) While the trade unions fixed minimum wage rates which reduced differentials much below the prewar levels, a comparative study by Bergson has shown that, in fact, earnings were similar in scale to those pertaining in the USA in 1904 (1944, p. 92). (The wage structure had seventeen divisions covering all non-manual and manual workers: the greatest differential between skilled and unskilled manual workers was 3½; the ratio of the highest basic salary to the lowest was 1:8. Bergson, 1944, p. 185.)

According to Soviet theory, egalitarianism would only be reached with full communism when all would receive 'according to their need'. In the early 1930s Stalin emphasised that, in the course of building socialism, workers could only be paid according to their work. He strongly opposed those who felt that under socialism wage differentials should be low:

> Equalitarianism owes its origin to the individual peasant type of mentality, the psychology of share and share alike, the psychology of primitive 'communism'. Equalitarianism has nothing in common with Marxist socialism. Only people who are unacquainted with Marxism can have the primitive notion that the Russian Bolsheviks want to pool all wealth and then share it out equally. That is the notion of people who have nothing in common with Marxism. (1955, pp. 120–1)

Consequently, much steeper differentials were introduced. In so far as earned income was concerned, in the USSR a similar pattern of wage inequality has been evolved as in capitalist societies (Dewar, 1962, p. 80).

There is some confusion between the notion of class in a Marxist sense and the prevalence of wage inequality. The abolition of classes does not necessarily entail the elimination of inequality in consumption. This highlights a division between, on the one hand, the social policy of modern social democratic politicians and Anarchists whose philosophy is strongly tempered with beliefs about distributive justice and that, on the other, of Marxists who emphasise class, ownership and political relations. For example, Crosland (1956) says: 'This belief in social equality, which has been the strongest ethical inspiration of virtually every socialist doctrine, still remains the most characteristic feature of socialist thought today' (p. 113). (See also Jenkins, 1952.) For Anarchist thinkers, Kropotkin (1888) asserts: 'We consider that an equitable organisation of society can only arise when every wage system is abandoned and when everyone contributing for the common well-being to the full extent of his capacities shall enjoy also from the common stock of society to the fullest possible extent of his needs' (p. 16). (See also Woodcock, 1962, p. 202.) At least Marxists in Lenin's mould regarded a concern for distributive equality to be petit-bourgeois. (See D. Lane, 1981, pp. 58–9.) Though Marx and Lenin saw communist society in its ultimate form as being without significant differential rewards.

What then were the principal characteristics of the early Soviet regime which are of relevance to this study? As Goldthorpe has suggested (1967, pp. 655–91), it is true that in a state-socialist society, the polity plays an important role in determining the class structure and the system of social stratification. The October Revolution destroyed some social groups (the aristocracy, large-scale private farmers, shopkeepers, financiers, the retainers on the large estates), it decisively strengthened the working class and secured the formation of other groups (collective farmers, commissars, the 'Soviet intelligentsia'). These were the effects of the work of the political leadership. But one must not naïvely think that, in this process, Soviet Communists designed a social structure in keeping with a political ideology. To quote from Marx, they made their own history not as they pleased, but 'under circumstances directly encountered, given and transmitted from the past'. The norms and values of different groups in the society set limits to the policies the political leadership could enforce. For example, at a very early stage after the Revolution, the expectations of skilled workers for higher remuneration were recognised and later, during the industrialisation process, the need for incentives to encourage workers into skilled and responsible jobs and to maintain a stable factory workforce resulted in even steeper wage differentials. But we can hardly infer from the early history of Soviet Russia that socialism is impracticable or utopian. Even less can this evidence be used to refute Marx's notion of an egalitarian communist form of social organisation. The reasons are clear. First, the economic basis inherited from Tsarist Russia had only just outgrown feudalism. Rather than introducing a socialist society qualitatively superior to capitalism, the Soviet regime in practice was faced with the construction of a technological basis similar to that of capitalist societies and it would be utopian to imagine that a socialist form of social relations could be constructed on it. Secondly, according to Marx, equality could only be achieved, and the dignity of manual labour ensured, when the division of labour was no longer necessary, when the material resources of production made such divisions no longer a requisite of the needs of industrial production. The structure of Soviet Russia in no way fulfilled this condition. The Russian Communists adapted Marxism to Soviet conditions. For Marx the 'dictatorship of the proletariat' was to be a relatively short period of rule, during which the working class (the majority) would preserve a social order superior to capitalism. In the Soviet Union the 'dictatorship of the proletariat' was an era of quite a different kind. The notion was utilised to justify the rule of the Communist Party which, at best, represented only the proletarian minority of the population. The Party used its power to transform the country, to carry out industrial growth, to introduce large-scale agriculture in the countryside. The policies had important effects on the structure of the population, they facilitated the growth of the working class and the movement of the population to the town. But rather than the consolidation of the rule of the proletariat as envisaged by Marx, the 'dictatorship of the proletariat' made the conditions in which a proletariat was created.

THE BUILDING OF SOCIALISM

At the beginning of this chapter, we noted four main historical phases in the history of Soviet society. Above we have seen what happened in the area of social stratification in the first two – the period of social revolution and the years of industrialisation. In this section we may now turn to the third phase, that of the building of socialism. Here we are discussing Soviet Russia; below (pp. 27–8), we consider other socialist societies.

For Marx, the 'dictatorship of the proletariat' was to be a short transitory period between the capitalist and communist epochs. In the Soviet Union, the 'dictatorship of the proletariat' lasted nineteen years, from 1917 to 1936. In the latter year the USSR was *officially* defined as a 'socialist' society: the first stage of the October Revolution, the 'dictatorship of the proletariat', had been consolidated. The previous ruling classes, it was argued, had been destroyed and the industrial basis of the USSR had been laid. Stalin believed that the economic changes which had taken place between 1924 and 1936 had 'destroyed and liquidated the exploitation of man by man', and had entailed the 'liquidation of all exploiting classes' (1967, pp. 141–2). He triumphantly declared that 'in principle, the first phase of communism, socialism, has been realised' (p. 149). In Soviet Marxist terms, it was argued that there was a complete correspondence between the productive relations and the character of forces of production in Soviet society. If we interpret Marxist theory literally, as Stalin did, after 1936 there could be no antagonistic 'classes' in the USSR for social classes are formed on the basis of ownership relations. As private ownership of the means of production had been progressively eliminated so, too, had been the property-owning classes, and since political power was held to derive from ownership, it followed that there could be no ruling and exploited classes. Socialist society, as defined by Stalin, was a harmonious society based on comradely co-operation.

The economic foundation of the USSR is the socialist system of economy and the socialist ownership of the instruments and means of production firmly established as a result of the abolition of the capitalist system of economy, private ownership of the instruments and means of production, and the exploitation of man by man. (*Constitution of the USSR*, 1936, article 4)

In the states of Eastern Europe the pattern was similar but not identical. The first official classification was that of a 'people's democracy'. This was a political order based on an alliance between several classes: there was no dominant class or ruling party – in theory. The dictatorship of the proletariat was proclaimed in the second stage and followed by the socialist formation which has been decreed in some but not all of the societies under consideration.

Let us leave aside until later criticisms of such views, which may be provided by alternative analyses of Soviet reality, in order to discuss for a moment the 'official' description of the social structure since 1936. This may be regarded as the transformation of Marxism into an ideology which justifies the rights of the Communist rulers, and seeks to make legitimate the social relations they created in Soviet Russia (see Lipset, 1969, pp. 208–9). As in original Marxism, social relations are regarded as being determined by class relations; and in Stalin's Russia there were the working class and the peasantry, and one social stratum: the intelligentsia. The Soviet *working class* was no longer a proletariat, because it was not exploited by a ruling class. On the contrary, on the basis of socialist property, it helped guide Soviet society to communism (Stalin, 1967, pp. 142–3). By the Soviet *peasantry*, Stalin referred to farmers engaged in agricultural production on collective farms. They were distinguished as a class from workers because they were in *co-operative* production. Though the land had been nationalised, they collectively owned its produce and the seeds used for production:

> In the collective farm, although the means of production (land, machines) do belong to the state, the product of production is the property of different collective farms, since the labour as well as the seed, is their own, while the land, which has been turned over to the collective farms in perpetual tenure, is used by them as their own property, in spite of the fact that they cannot sell, lease or mortgage it. (Stalin, 1952, p. 19)

The essential class difference between the workers and collective-farm peasants was one of ownership relations. Even though they did not own the large-scale machinery which was then kept under state control in machine tractor stations, the peasants still had collective ownership over at least part of the means of production. The working class, on the other hand, were employed in nationalised state-run enterprises and their work was planned, regulated and defined by the government, whereas these aspects of labour in the collective farm were under the jurisdiction of the general farm meeting.

In addition to the two classes described above, there was also the *intelligentsia* which was a stratum technically part of the working class and composed of non-manual rather than manual workers. Stalin included in this category a wide range of employees – engineering and technical, those 'on the cultural front' and 'workers by brain [*sluzhashchie*] in general' (1967, p. 145). This stratum embraced those in the strategic commanding and creative roles in society, as well as the more menial clerical and administrative jobs. The chief distinction between manual workers and the intelligentsia then is based on the role each group plays in the social organisation of labour. These two classes and one stratum have, in Soviet theory, a common interest, together 'in one harness' they carry out 'the building of a new classless socialist society'.

These ideas, articulated by Stalin in the 1930s, form the ideological basis on which the notion of socialist society is conceived of in the USSR. The second and higher phase of the building of communist society, or 'developed socialist society' in Brezhnev's terms, entails a 'state of the whole people, expressing the will and interests of the workers, peasants, and intelligentsia, the working people of all the nations and nationalities of the country' (*Constitution of the USSR*, 1977, article 1). The 1977 Constitution replaced that of 1936. For complete text, see D. Lane (1978).

The Soviet Union has provided the model for other states which I would classify as 'state socialist'. These societies have not followed the course of the USSR as defined above. Rather than being self-defined in their formative years as a 'dictatorship of the proletariat', the official classification has been that of a 'people's democracy'. This was a political order based on an alliance between several classes. The 'dictatorship of the proletariat' was declared after it. The third stage was the socialist which usually is considered to be the social form of a society with a large proportion of its industry and trade being state owned and having collectivised agriculture. The diachronic stages defined above are then telescoped into a much shorter period of time.

In the Chinese People's Republic, the first article of the 1954 Constitution defines it as 'a people's democratic state led by the working class and based on the alliance of workers and peasants', it allowed 'ownership by individual working people and capitalist ownership' (article 5); the law protected the 'right of peasants to own land and other means of production' (article 8), and 'the right of capitalists to own means of production and capital' (article 10). The Chinese Constitution of 1975 presents a radically changed picture. The People's Republic is regarded as 'a socialist state of proletarian dictatorship'. No rights to capitalist forms of ownership are mentioned and the main categories of ownership are socialist ownership by the whole people and socialist collective ownership by working people.

It is important to emphasise the fact that cultural and economic conditions vary tremendously between what I have defined generically as 'state-socialist societies'. In Poland, for instance, not only is the class of private entrepreneurs more important and a non-collectivised peasantry remains, but the Catholic Church still retains the allegiance of a sizeable part of the population and the intelligentsia keeps much of its prestige and lifestyle inherited from pre-socialist Poland. (See Szczepanski, 1970, ch. 6.)

Social Change: Non-Antagonistic Contradictions

From a knowledge of Marxist theory, one might expect that social change would continue until a classless society had been achieved. Stalin indeed said that the distance between these social groups would be reduced more and more (1967, p. 146). Here, however, we have a problem: in Marxist theory, change is the result of a dialectical process, it is a synthesis of thesis and antithesis. But how could one have a dialectical synthesis in a society characterised by social harmony, in which all antagonistic class contradictions had been resolved? Stalin did not face up to this problem when he discussed the class structure of Soviet society in 1936, though he noted that the 'economic . . . and political contradictions between these social groups will recede and will wipe themselves out'. Later attempts during Stalin's lifetime to discuss the problem of contradictions were not very penetrating. The view generally held was that put forward in a leading article in *Pod znamenem marksizma*: 'the complete harmony between the forces of production and production relations of socialism does not presuppose, but *excludes* contradictions between them' (cited by Shtraks, 1966, pp. 32-3).

There are two theoretical attempts to resolve the problem just described. The first is that adopted by anti-Soviet Marxists. They consider that the class struggle and irreconcilable contradictions persist in the USSR. We shall postpone our discussion of these views until later (see Chapter 5, pp. 126-51). A second explanation is that favoured by Soviet Marxist-Leninists themselves: 'non-antagonistic' contradictions, they say, will persist in Soviet society until the final stage, communist society, is reached.

The latter thesis involves a distinction between a non-antagonistic and an antagonistic contradiction. A non-antagonistic contradiction is one which may be resolved by quantitative change, whereas an antagonistic contradiction can only be resolved by a qualitative one. In the first case a contradiction may be resolved *within the parameters* of a given social system, in the second case, the nature of the social system itself must be changed (Shtraks, 1966, pp. 32-3). A non-antagonistic contradiction would involve adjustments between groups or institutions whereas an antagonistic one could only be resolved by the formation of a new social order (capitalism, communism).

Another way to look at the problem is to consider the relation between basis and superstructure. The *basis* is composed of two elements: the forces of production (tools and technology) and production relations (property relations). In a state-socialist society the relationship between these two elements of the basis is a harmonious one whereas in capitalist society such relations are antagonistic – the capitalist property relations are a fetter on the development of the forces of production. The *superstructure* is a set of institutions (educational, ideological, political, social) which are functionally linked to the basis. Thus, it is argued, the sources of non-antagonistic contradictions in state-socialist society may be found either in the basis due to the persistence of pre-socialist technological forms, or in a possible incongruity between basis and superstructure, for example administrative institutions (such as Khrushchev's regional economic councils) may be inappropriate to the productive forces or there may be 'remnants' of bourgeois ideology – religion, nationality (Shtraks, 1966, pp. 77–8).

In my view, it is confusing and inappropriate to use the term 'non-antagonistic contradiction'. The definition of 'contradiction' involves the antagonism of thesis and antithesis, and its resolution by a qualitative change in which the opposing elements find their synthesis at a new and higher level. The dialectic entails a process which is self-sustaining. But in the official Soviet theory, set out above, we have no such opposition, resolution and synthesis. As a social process, 'non-antagonistic contradictions' are externally regulated by the political system, and would more appropriately be referred to as 'incongruencies' or 'dysfunctions'. From the viewpoint of the official model, one might say that in Soviet society certain values, groups and practices are at variance with the central value system and the dominant social, economic and political institutions: in other words, their existence is *dysfunctional* to the attainment of goals that are defined by the political élites. In Soviet terms these are either remnants from the old pre-socialist society or else they have an exogenous origin in the decadent capitalist order. Social change takes place not by the resolution of internal contradictions involving qualitative leaps, such as that from capitalism to socialism, but rather by guided growth. As a Soviet writer says of the social structure: 'Under the conditions of socialism, where there is no state of class opposites, the remains of social inequality in significant part are connected with the character of labour and the cultural-technical level of the mass of workers' (*Problemy izmeneniya sotsial'noy struktury Sovetskogo obshchestva*, 1968, p. 61).

The same writer defines four main areas of social inequality. First, there are distinctions based on class relationships – (i.e. peasantry and working class). Secondly, there are differences between rural and urban populations. Thirdly, distinctions persist between manual and non-manual labour. Finally, there are differences associated with various trades, skills and incomes (Glezerman, 1968). These four distinctions provide the basis for most Soviet sociologists' descriptions of social stratification in modern Russia (the epoch of the building of communism) which will be examined in the next chapter.

A more sociological analysis of the interests and contradictions in socialist society, with reference to contemporary Poland, has been put forward by Wlodzimierz Wesolowski (1979). He distinguishes sharply between interests derived from class position, in a Marxist sense, and those derived from the place one occupies in 'the social division of labour'. Following Lenin, Wesolowski views classes as 'groups of persons where one can live from labour of another, where one can appropriate the fruits of the labour of the other' (p. 103). The nationalisation of private property, argues Wesolowski, 'abolishes the class structure as conceived above . . . There occurs the abolition of the basic class relationship typical of capitalist society. The workers . . . cease to be a class in the old sense of the word' (ibid.). While class interests gradually wither away in (state) socialist society, Wesolowski notes that social differentiation, or social stratification, remains: various attributes such as nature of work, income, education, prestige 'retain in socialism an "autonomous" existence' (p. 114). However, unlike under capitalism where class position, political power, income, status and education are highly congruent, in socialist states a 'decomposition' takes place where, for instance, high income may compensate for low status. Such stratification of groups may give rise to conflicts of interest between them – which may be resolved without changing the structure of society. With the maturation of socialist states, and with the greater material abundance which they ensure, Wesolowski predicts a reduction in the occurrence of conflict over the unequal distribution of goods. Here the antithesis between 'freedom' and 'equality' is resolved, for greater material wealth gives greater possibilities for freedom of choice. Neo-conservatives, however, would take exception to this conclusion and would argue that a tension exists, even under socialism between equality and achievement and that the emphasis on

31

equality, with its consequences for the growth of state power, is a significant limit on human achievement, on regard for merit and hence on individual freedom (see Connor, 1979, ch. 1).

It is with respect to authority that Wesolowski, like Lenin, parts company with many libertarian socialists. Even in socialist society, the need for organisation calls for authority and for superordinate-subordinate relationships. Quoting Engels with approval, he asserts that 'Wanting to abolish authority in large scale industry is tantamount to wanting to abolish industry itself . . . A certain authority and a certain subordination are things which impose themselves on us independently of all social organisation together with the material conditions under which we produce and make products circulate' (1979, p. 98). A consequence of socialist construction is 'the emergence of a whole hierarchy of command positions'. Stratification by authority is a 'necessity resulting from the fact of communal human existence' (p. 99).

The views we have discussed so far constitute the 'official' version of social reality: they emphasise consensus rather than conflict and hierarchy rather than dichotomy. It need hardly be said that other writers on contemporary socialist states have strenuously attacked this image of social harmony and have argued that, on the contrary, the pattern of social relations is characterised by an opposition, sometimes manifest but more often latent, between conflicting groups. Such theories have in common the notion that inequality and stratification under state socialism are in essence of a *political* nature. Rather than hierarchy and political control being legitimate in defining the interests of the working class, as suggested by Wesolowski, these critics view the holders of power to be exercising it in their own right, and acting in an exploitative way over the masses. Also, rather than the 'decomposition' of power position, income and status, the ruling élite or class is seen to be strengthening its domination along these dimensions. While these critics often disagree about the particular configuration of the ruling groups and about whether they are best described as classes or elites, they do agree that one social group rules over another and that the dominant group exploits the masses.

One type of conflict theory uses the terminology of class and is considered, by its protagonists at any rate, to be Marxian in orientation. A second approach, while retaining some of the trappings of class conflict, focuses on authority relations and the role of bureaucracy. A third type of theory defines conflict in terms of élite and mass and is explicitly anti-Marxist in its viewpoint. Like Marxism, these are theories of society which embrace many aspects of the social system in addition to social stratification. Here the main problem with which we shall be concerned is the nature of socio-political stratification in a system where, as Marxist–Leninists maintain, private ownership of the means of production has been abolished. But we shall postpone further discussion of these views until Chapter 5, until we have considered the forms of inequality and their extent in socialist societies.

2 Social Inequality: Soviet Sociology's Interpretation of the Social Structure

At the beginning of Chapter 1, we noted four main historical phases in the history of Soviet society. Above we saw what happened in the area of social stratification during the first three – the period of social revolution, the years of industrialisation and the first phase of the 'building of socialism'. In this chapter we shall focus on what Soviet philosophers and sociologists call the period of the building of communism (the post-1956 period) and we shall be more concerned with description than theory. But it is important to note here that 'the facts' about societies have not been collected independently of the ways in which sociologists and others conceive (or desire) society to be arranged. In describing and explaining social stratification sociologists are often influenced by ideologies of social stratification. Established political élites encourage the propagation of views which justify their own power and the existing state of inequality, whereas revolutionaries express quite opposite convictions. Furthermore, a ruling party or political élite may not only legitimate its power by reference to a theory of society justifying inequality but it may direct research into socially (and politically) 'legitimate' topics and consequently in such societies it is sometimes impossible to investigate certain 'unauthorised' topics in the fields of class, power, social inequality or social relations. (I have in mind the absence of published studies of attitudes towards the political leadership, or to the authority of the Communist Party. In the West 'corporate image research' on the esteem of large corporations and their profits is done privately and not published; in Britain, sociologists have paid scant attention to popular attitudes towards the monarchy and the public expenditure it incurs.) Theorists who emphasise class or group conflict are therefore at a considerable disadvantage in the ideological struggle over defining the nature of Soviet society because Soviet sociologists, when publishing empirical data, tend to select facts which do not vitiate the 'official' ideology of social harmony. In other state-socialist societies, such as Poland and Hungary, where sociologists have had a freer hand to define their own interests, research has been more penetrating and in the chapters following this one, Soviet research will be supplemented by work carried out in Eastern Europe.

The main characteristic of Soviet research into social stratification in Soviet society is that while inequality, as such, is studied it is denied that such inequality gives rise to exclusive socio-economic groups. By 'inequality' we mean that certain commodities or values, such as income, consumer goods and education are unequally distributed among groups of the population. Such groups may be described as being more or less privileged or underprivileged. But, as Soviet sociologists point out, persons may have very unequal incomes but their respect for each other and the deference of third parties to them may be quite unrelated to their income. Sociologists in state-socialist societies would also concede that there are important differences between socio-economic groups, that occupations vary greatly in their 'prestige' and that lifestyles and 'consciousness' differ (Shkaratan and Rukavishnikov, 1977; Popova and Moin, 1979, pp. 83–90; and Wesolowski, 1979, pp. 104–9). Stratification exists within the class groupings of workers and collective farmers. The main kinds of inequality which Soviet sociologists have studied may be summarised under three headings noted in Chapter 1: inequalities between the collective-farm peasantry and the working class, between town and country and between manual and non-manual labour.

THE WORKING CLASS AND COLLECTIVE-FARM PEASANTRY

The working class is given pride of place in the Soviet sociologist's description of the Soviet social structure. It is 'the creator, the builder of a new society of labour'. It has as its aim the 'liquidation of class differences, the creation of a classless communist society' (Semenov, 1968, p. 6). The 'working class' which is divided into manual and non-manual workers is defined to include all those (and their families) employed in state and public institutions. In the 1979 census the working class comprises 85·1 per cent of the population (including 25·1 per cent non-manual workers) and the collective-farm peasantry 14·9 per cent ('Zhenshchiny v SSSR', 1981, p. 66). The working class, it should be noted, includes those employed in agriculture in state, as distinct from collective, farms. In 1978 14·3 million men and women were engaged in collective-farm agriculture and 11·8 million in state farming. In total, approximately 21·5 per cent of the occupied labour force was engaged in agriculture (Tsentral'noe, 1979, pp. 287, 86, 363). The Soviet working class, in Soviet ideology, is not 'superior' to the peasantry in the sense of being economically or socially privileged, it is at a socially more advanced stage by virtue of ownership relations and is destined to take the lead in building a communist society.

Whereas 'the worker' is employed by the state and does not own or market any of his produce, the 'collective farmer' is engaged in co-operative production and his income is dependent on the produce which is farmed and marketed co-operatively by the collective farm to which the government has leased the land 'in perpetuity'. All farmers (state and collective) have the right to farm an individual plot, the produce of which may be sold on the free agricultural market. This small-scale production perpetuates the more traditional peasant mode of production. While the total area cultivated is small the share of the plots in total agricultural output in 1979 came to 59 per cent of the potatoes, 31 per cent of vegetables and 33 per cent of the eggs (Tsentral'noe, 1980, p. 222). Between 1965 and 1979, the area under private cultivation rose from 6·6 million hectares to 8·39 million, though between 1970 and 1978 the index of private production (mainly of meat, milk and fowl) remained fairly constant (Tsentral'noe, 1979, pp. 196–7; Tsentral'noe, 1980, p. 237; Staroverov, 1978, p. 141). The collective farmer on a collective farm may be contrasted with the agricultural worker on a state farm. The state farm is organised like a factory by a ministry which owns the tools and produce and which appoints the farm director. The workers on state farms receive regular wages, they may be members of trade unions and they have the same rights to welfare services as men employed in other industries. Indeed, the state farm is conceived of by Soviet theorists as a kind of agricultural factory, in which work is more mechanised, educational and cultural standards are higher than on collective farms and the men employed regard themselves as 'workers' rather than as smallholders working co-operatively.

Until 1966 collective farmers received wages depending on the number of their labour days and the income of the farm. Their pay was irregular – sometimes quarterly in arrears. In the 1970s this system was changed and now in most areas collective farmers have similar wage rates to workers in state farms. Similarly, social security used to be provided by payments from the farm's own funds – not state funds – but nowadays state social security is increasingly available to collective farmers (see below Table 2.3). On attaining adulthood, collective farmers receive, like a state farmer, an internal passport and they, too, are eligible to join a trade union which gives various security benefits and pension rights.

Both Soviet and Western commentators agree that the Soviet collective farmer is not like the peasant in other parts of the world. As a unit of production, the 'ideal-typical' peasant household takes decisions over planting and harvesting and it is mostly dependent for its subsistence on goods produced on its own land. It is not only an economic unit but also a system of authority and welfare. The peasant family is normally patriarchal and its functions include both the socialisation of children and provision for the old and infirm. Perhaps most important of all, the 'typical peasant' is held to have a close attachment to the soil; for him husbandry is a way of life with its own primordial rhythm. The Soviet peasantry, however, differs in important respects from this pattern. The activity of the collective farm must be 'in conformity' with the general economic plan. The farm must provide foodstuffs and raw materials (flax, cotton, etc.) essential to the needs of the economy. Therefore, it is the collective farm rather than the peasant household as such which takes decisions about agricultural production; and the product mix and methods of the collective farm are, in turn, closely supervised by the Ministry of Agriculture. Furthermore, the collective-farm household does not receive collectively payment according to the work its members provide on the farm but rather the latter receive payments as individuals. This has an important effect on family structure because the peasant wife and the children of working age have separate and independent sources of income which militate against forms of patriarchal authority. Moreover, the organisation of education by the state also has the effect of weakening the family's socialisation role. But perhaps the most important factor in the life of the Soviet peasant is political: while all peasants face political demands or pressures from the wider society, which may take the form of claims for economic surplus (in goods or labour power), the Soviet collective farm has within it the influence of the political ruling class in the form of the Communist Party branch. This plays a most important part in the selection of the farm chairman who is formally elected by the members of the farm. Because production is in co-operative (not state) ownership the Soviet collective farmer is regarded from the Soviet viewpoint as not being fully emancipated from the fetters of the capitalist mode of production. He still needs to be led, as it were, along the path to communism by the working class. 'Without the aid of the progressive class of society [i.e. the working class], the peasantry by itself may not achieve communism and may not surmount the remains of past petty-bourgeois narrow-mindedness' (*Problemy izmeneniya sotsial'noy struktury Sovetskogo obshchestva*, 1968, p. 69).

However, the liquidation of these differences between the working class and the peasantry is not envisaged to occur through the process of class struggle. Change is conceived of in essentially non-dialectic terms in the form of a 'drawing together' of the collective-farm peasantry and working class in the process of building communism. It is expected that changes in the 'material base of the village' will affect the character of collective-farm production and the social relations which rest upon it. The growing mechanisation of agriculture and the application of modern methods in the collective farm bring about changes in the occupational structure as illustrated by Table 2.1. The numbers of collective farmers engaged in traditional peasant work of field labour has fallen considerably: in 1975 less than half (40·4 per cent) of the workforce was made up of unskilled and

Table 2.1   Occupational Structure of the Collective-Farm
Peasantry

	1960		1975	
Skilled manual workers	8·4		16·9	
Skilled non-manual workers	28·2		42·7	
Unskilled and semi-skilled workers	63·4		40·4	
of which are engaged:				
in animal husbandry	–	7·9	–	4·7
in crop growing	–	53·2	–	34·0
(residual)	–	(2·3)	–	(1·7)
	100·0		100·0	

Source: Adapted from Staroverov (1977, p. 60).

semi-skilled toilers. Concurrent with these changes have come
improvements in the educational levels of collective farmers.

Those doing the more skilled jobs have a different attitude
towards work than the unskilled and this is illustrated by the data
in Table 2.2, which is based on a survey of 872 collective farmers

Table 2.2   'What Do You Like in Your Work?' (In Percentages of
Respondents)

Aspect of work	1 'Village intelligentsia and white collar'	2 Workers using machines (Mekhani-zatory)	3 Skilled manual workers	4 Semi-skilled and unskilled workers
The great social significance of my work	68·8	64·8	62·6	43·5
High wages	1·5	11·8	27·7	4·1
The possibility to increase qualifications	9·8	13·8	7·0	4·8
Good relationships with other workers	29·4	49·3	32·0	30·2
Good relationships on the part of the management	18·9	21·5	20·0	9·5
Work requires thought, demands intelligence	33·5	36·5	9·5	11·7
The good organisation of labour	7·6	7·3	7·2	2·7

Source: Vorontsov (1980, p. 84).

in Smolensk, Leningrad and Pskov districts of the RSFSR in 1978. It may be observed that groups 1 and 2 scored more highly than 3 and 4 in relationship to the social significance of work, the possibility to increase qualifications and the intellectual demands of work. The lower number of responses from the unskilled and semi-skilled collective farmers probably reflects a lower level of social consciousness.

A rise in the productivity of labour will also make possible the reduction of the farm workforce and the migration of the rural population to urban centres. All these developments will tend to make the structure of collective farms more and more like industrial enterprises. Forms of joint production between collective farms and state enterprises are planned to speed up the division of labour and undermine the 'co-operative' mode of production. Through this process, the collective-farm co-operative form of property will 'grow over' into communist property. The conditions of labour are coming to approximate those of the working class as regular monthly wages and the state provision of a wide range of social services (free meals, children's nurseries, social insurance, state pensions) become more widespread.

There are still, however, important differences between the collective farmers and the industrial working class. The data in Table 2.3 may be used to illustrate both the convergence of living standards and the differences which remain between the two groups. (For a detailed description of changes from 1960 to 1974, see McAuley, 1979, ch. 2.) The major differences lie in the sources of income: while income from 'the collective farm' (which might be conceived to be analogous to 'wages' for the industrial worker) has risen from 39·7 per cent of the collective farmers' income in 1940 to 44.5 per cent in 1978, in the latter year, a quarter of total income still originated from personal enterprise, that is, consumption of foodstuffs and sales on the collective-farm market. The great disparity between industrial workers and collective farmers with respect to state services which existed in 1940 had been almost eliminated by 1978. Consideration of the figures for 'outlays', however, shows that consumption of socio-cultural and welfare services is still very much less for the collective farmer than for the industrial

Table 2.3 *Income and Expenditure of Families of Industrial Workers and Collective Farmers (Percentages)*

	1940		1965		1978	
	Indus-trial Worker	Collec-tive Farmer	Indus-trial Worker	Collec-tive Farmer	Indus-trial Worker	Collec-tive Farmer
Total family income	100	100	100	100	100	100
Income from collective farm	–	39·7	–	40·0	–	44·5
Wages of members of family	71·3	5·8	73·1	7·4	74·3	8·7
Pensions, grants, other services provided for (e.g. education)	14·5	4·9	22·8	14·2	22·7	20·4
Income from personal enterprise	9·2	48·3	1·7	36·5	0·8	25·2
Income from other sources	5·0	1·3	2·4	1·9	2·2	1·2
Outlays as percentage of total income	100	100	100	100	100	100
Food	53·8	67·3	37·9	45·2	32·0	34·4
Purchases of textiles, clothing, footwear	11·1	10·9	13·9	13·7	15·7	15·6
Purchases of fuel	1·2	3·8	0·4	2·0	0·2	1·8
Purchase of other goods	1·7	1·2	6·1	4·2	6·6	5·9
On social-cultural and welfare services	17·5	4·4	24·2	12·5	22·8	14·9
of which education, medical and other free goods	9·0	3·4	13·8	10·0	13·6	11·7
of which payment for flats, communal services and maintenance of private houses	2·7	–	2·5	–	2·5	–
Savings	4·8	6·9	3·4	12·1	7·2	13·1
Taxes	4·1	1·4	7·1	1·4	8·7	1·3
Other outgoings	5·8	4·1	7·0	8·9	6·8	13·0

Source: Adapted from Tsentral'noe (1979, pp. 391–2), based on surveys of 62,000 families.

worker. (Only 14·9 per cent of consumption compared to 22·8 per cent.) The equalisation of living standards is indexed by the proportion of expenditure going on food: for collective farmers the share was 34·4 per cent in 1978 compared to 32 per cent for industrial workers, whereas in 1940 the figures were 67·3 per cent and 53·8 per cent respectively. These, of course, are proportions of outgoings, the real income of the families of collective farmers in 1978 came to 88 per cent of that of those of manual and non-manual workers; in 1965 it was only 75 per cent (Tsentral'noe, 1979, p. 387).

The discussion so far has focused on the *class* difference between collective farmers and workers in terms of the Soviet definition of the relevance of collective-farm property. There are, however, many other significant aspects of social stratification which affect a whole range of rural inhabitants and it is to these that we now turn.

TOWN AND COUNTRY

At first sight, the merging of the collective-farm peasantry with the working class would appear to entail the elimination of differences between farmer and industrial worker. In fact, town/country distinctions go much deeper than those between collective farmer and industrial worker. The low population density of rural Russia gives unequal facilities to the large number of people who live in the countryside. In 1981, 37 per cent of the population was classified as rural. Because the rural population is thinly spread, the provision of the same level of social and cultural services as in the town is not economically feasible and there has been a tendency to concentrate services in urban centres. The town thus becomes a cultural and social centre, housing communications, theatres, specialised shops, hospitals and the higher educational establishments on which the village becomes heavily dependent. The standard of living is also generally lower in the village than in the town. A rough index is given by the fact that in 1978 39 per cent of the population which was engaged in industry and building received 65·6 per cent of the national income, whereas the share of the 21 per cent of the population employed in agriculture was only 17·5 per cent (Tsentral'noe, 1979, pp. 363, 386).

Sociologists have described inequalities between town and country in several different ways. First, in the villages a much higher proportion of labour is occupied in manual work and conversely a lower proportion is in non-manual. These occupational differences may be illustrated by data collected in the census of 1970: of the urban population, 65·6 per cent of the labour force was engaged in jobs requiring predominantly manual labour (in 1959 the comparative figure was 71·3 per cent), in the countryside the figures were 84·1 per cent (88·7 in 1959) (Tsentral'noe, 1973, Vol. 6, p. 7). Of the village workforce, the largest single group (40 per cent in 1975) was that of unskilled or semi-skilled workers in material production (66·5 per cent in 1959) (Staroverov, 1977, p. 56).

Secondly, in the countryside educational standards are lower and social services worse than in the town. In 1979 for every 1,000 people living in towns there were 93 with higher education, whereas in the villages the comparable figure was only 25 (*Naselenie*, 1980, p. 21). The numbers of people employed in various aspects of social and communal services such as education, health, public catering and welfare services, are much lower per capita in the villages than in the towns, even if we bear in mind that urban areas provide services such as hospitalisation and higher education for the villages as well as for their own inhabitants.

Thirdly, there is more direct evidence of the cultural impoverishment of rural life. Table 2.4 distinguishes between collective farm, state farm, village settlement and town district, and shows the proportion of families who own radios and television sets, the size of their personal libraries and the number of their subscriptions to journals. By all three measures the cultural level of the town is clearly superior. We see that 59 per cent of town families had television, 25·7 per cent had a library with more than a hundred books and 36·5 per cent subscribed to more than three papers and journals. By comparison the figures for collective-farm families were much lower – 0, 0·3 per cent and 13·2 per cent respectively. In a survey of leisure-time activities of collective farmers conducted in the 1970s, it was found that 51 per cent 'read literature', 35 per cent regularly visit the cinema and the same proportion regularly look at the television, and 18 per cent regularly listen to the radio (Simush, 1976, p. 134).

Fourthly, the influence of traditional values is greater in the

Table 2.4   *Cultural Level of Urban and Rural Population (1963)*

	Collective farm	State farm	Village settlement	Town district
Families surveyed *N*	371	836	1,040	315
Percentages of families having:				
Radio relay points	48·0	35·8	11·0	20·7
Radio sets	34·8	43·9	73·0	78·1
Television sets			22·0	59·0
Personal libraries				
1–10 books	15·1	5·0	8·2	4·7
11–50	13·5	22·5	26·0	33·2
51–100	3·5	3·8	8·3	19·3
More than 100	0·3	2·7	5·4	25·7
Subscriptions to papers and journals				
1	28·0	29·2	39·0	19·6
2–3	38·3	33·8	31·0	33·2
More than 3	13·2	7·7	5·0	36·5

Source: Klassy, sotsial'nye sloi i gruppy v SSSR (1968, p. 127).

village than the town. Not only is the influence of media somewhat less, but the socialising role of the family is greater than in the town. This probably accounts for the persistence of traditional values in the countryside. In a study of several rural regions in the USSR, Arutyunyan (1971, p. 188) found that believers in God were distributed as follows: of the men, 28 per cent in the collective farms, 10 per cent in the state farms and only 8 per cent in the industrial enterprise; for women the figures were 62 per cent, 39 per cent and 35 per cent respectively. Christel Lane's comprehensive study of the Soviet literature on religiosity shows that Christian believers are concentrated disproportionately among the lowly educated rural population (C. Lane, 1978, pp. 226–7).

Fifthly, the political orientation of the collective farmer is held to be differentiated from the politically dominant urban working class. The relations between these two classes are complex and cannot be fully treated here. In theory, there is a *smychka* or alliance between the two classes but the lower level of social consciousness and the role of private husbandry, discussed above, leads to lower identification with the values of a communist state. Formal Party membership is one, albeit imperfect, index of allegiance. In 1981, 12·8 per cent of Party membership were collective farmers, a lower proportion than in the population as a whole (i.e. about 14·8 per cent). The membership of collective farmers, however, is growing: a figure of 541,800 in 1946 rose to 1·4 million in 1973, and 2·2 million in 1981, and the average size of Party primary group rose between 1946 and 1973 from 11 to 49 (Simush, 1976, pp. 43, 188–9). The strengthening of the Party in the countryside is seen as going hand in hand with the 'merging' of the collective farmers into the working class. Between 1976 and 1980, of new collective-farmer entrants to the Party, 31·5 per cent were workers with machines and 'specialists' made up another 20·9 per cent (*Partiynaya zhizn'*, 1981, no. 14, p. 15). Clearly, one would need to know more about actual political orientations of collective farmers before one could conclusively talk about a 'merging' of these two social groups.

We might, however, make a number of at least tentative conclusions about the changing nature of the peasantry in the Soviet Union. It seems to me that the old traditional parochial peasant of Tsarist Russia is a dying breed. The spread of education, of the mass media, of modern technology, of modern working methods is having a debilitating effect on the old peasant consciousness. The urban areas are having a 'modernising' influence on the rural population. It would be too strong to say that traditional ways do not continue, but they remain in an attenuated form shared more by the older, female and lowly educated country-dwellers. One might agree with Hill that the term 'peasantry', in the sense of a distinct social group with particular characteristics to a high degree, 'has not applied [in the USSR] for some time' (Hill, 1975, p. 127).

It is impossible here to discuss the affinity of the above description with the peasantry in other state-socialist societies. One may highlight the fact that in the process of industrial-isation, urban areas are often under-capitalised and the phenomenon of peasant-worker or worker-peasant arises which entails dual occupations and regular commuting of peasants to the town. Such strata cannot easily be fitted into the scheme of Soviet sociologists studied above. (On Poland, see P. Lewis, 1973.) And neither can be the structural conditions in Poland where half-hearted collectivisation has resulted in only about 1 per cent of farms being collectivised and small-scale private enterprise continues.

MANUAL AND NON-MANUAL LABOUR

According to the Marxist theory of capitalist society, the executive, administrative and superior technical personnel occupy a peculiar place in the system of class relations. While such strata do not by objective class position form part of the bourgeoisie (they do not necessarily own the means of production), they are closely identified with it. They serve the interests of capitalism and their subjective class interest is perceived to lie with the bourgeoisie.

Soviet sociologists deny that any similar antagonistic relationship exists between manual workers and such executive and administrative strata in the USSR on the grounds that there is no private property and because 'a significant part of the intelligentsia [is made up] of men who started as workers and of the children of workers'. The differences between manual and non-manual strata are created fundamentally by the division of labour. As Shkaratan has put it: 'The social division of labour inherent in socialism . . . emerges as the foundation of actual inequality of groups of workers who, owing to the operation of the law of distribution according to work, end up with unequal shares in the national income of society' (1973, p. 13). Manual and non-manual workers perform different roles in the 'social organization of labour'; manual workers work mainly with their hands and non-manual predominantly with their brains. 'Engineers and technicians are occupied in the administration of production, workers are engaged chiefly in executive labour' (Semenov, 1962, p. 249). The role of these strata in the production process results in inequalities between them in income and consumption, in their cultural and technical levels and in their standard of living. Soviet sociologists perceive social relations in objective rather than subjective terms, recognising as significant the division of labour and differential levels of consumption. Hence, in their approach, such writers share a common political and ideological stance to social stratification *under socialism*, as do functionalists to capitalism – inequalities are linked to qualifications and levels of skill. They take a diametrically opposite position to such Western Marxists as Wright who minimise skill as an objective factor differentiating various types of worker (manual and non-manual) (Wright, 1976).

The broad classification of non-manual employees, or brain-workers, may be broken down into a number of distinct groups differentiated according to character of work. The total number of employed non-manuals in the USSR in 1979 was 38·8 million. The 'socialist intelligentsia' proper, is defined as those possessing higher education (18 million in 1979) and those with secondary specialist education (23·4 million in 1979) (census data). Within the category of intelligentsia come the leaders of government departments (211,000 in 1970) Party and trade-union leaders (195,000) and enterprise chiefs (1·6 million in 1970), those engaged in higher education and culture (art, literature, the press) (1,049,000), and the largest group, the 'upper technical intelligentsia' which was over 3 million strong. (Data derived from 1970 census, Tsentral'noe, 1973, Vol. 7, pp. 20–1. These figures refer to people occupying the given roles, they do not necessarily possess higher or specialist educational qualifications.) At the other end of the spectrum of the non-manual group performing more routine and less theoretically demanding work are clerks, draughtsmen and teachers in infant schools.

Soviet sociologists distinguish between eight broad occupational strata: unskilled and semi-skilled manuals (11·8 per cent of the urban population), skilled manual workers (46·5 per cent), manual workers with very high levels of skill (4 per cent), unskilled non-manual employees (8 per cent), skilled non-manuals with specialist secondary education (18·2 per cent), skilled non-manuals with higher education (6·8 per cent), non-manuals engaged in very highly skilled creative work (1·9 per cent), non-manuals doing highly skilled administrative work (2·8 per cent) (Shkaratan, Filippova and Demidova, 1980, p. 32).

Table 2.5 Some Aspects of the Social Structure of Leningrad Engineering Workers (1965 and 1970)

Group of workers	(A) 1965				(B) 1970		
	Education (years)	Wages, roubles (monthly)	Party/ Komsomol membership (%)	Participation in voluntary work (%)	Party/ Komsomol membership (%)	Years of education	Wages, roubles (monthly)
(1) Management (factory directors, shop superintendents)	13·6	172·9	60·8	84·2	–	13·4	191·0
(2) Non-manual workers in highly skilled technical-scientific jobs (designers)	14·0	127·0	40·2	70·4	–	14·1	133·0
(3) Skilled non-manual workers (technologists, bookkeepers)	12·5	109·8	42·8	82·4	–	12·8	131·0
(4) Highly skilled workers in jobs with mental and manual functions (tool setters)	8·8	129·0	37·6	79·2	44·3	9·8	142·0
(5) Skilled workers of superior manual work (fitters, welders)	8·3	120·0	37·4	60·7	34·6	8·7	140·0
(6) Skilled manual workers (machine-tool operators, press operators)	8·2	107·5	39·5	54·3	35·4	8·4	14·2
(7) Non-manual workers of medium skill (inspection and office workers)	9·1	83·6	27·1	54·5	–	–	90·0
(8) Unskilled manual workers	6·5	97·5	13·8	35·1	12·2	5·6	106·0

Sources: (A) Adapted from Shkaratan (1967, p. 36); (B) from Trufanov (1973, pp. 61–2).

Manual workers are also differentiated by the level of skill on which their rates of pay are calculated, there being six grades of pay in most industries. The bottom grades of lowly skilled manual and non-manual workers in fact have similar pay scales, though the non-manual worker has a higher level of education. Differences between various strata of the manual and non-manual working class have been delineated by the research of Shkaratan (1967) and Trufanov for 1970 (the latter cited by Yanowitch, 1977, p. 34). This is summarised on Table 2.5. Shkaratan divides the working class by occupation, education, wages, Party/Komsomol (Young Communist League) membership and participation in voluntary work. The 'objective' differences are clearly shown on the table. In 1965 education ranges from 6·5 years to 14 years (groups 8 and 2), income from 83·6 roubles to 172·9 roubles (groups 7 and 1), Party membership varies from 13·8 per cent to 60·8 per cent (groups 8 and 1), and participation from 35·1 per cent to 84·2 per cent. The pay of group 7 (non-manual workers), it may be noted, in both years is lower than that of the manual group 8, though the level of education is higher. Also the educational level of group 3 is higher than that of the formally non-manual group 4, though the rankings of earnings is reversed.

Soviet writers, then, have a picture of three main groups (non-manuals, manual workers and peasants) each one being subdivided into objective strata based mainly on skill and type of occupation. Inequalities between them, it is believed, will decrease with the development of the productive forces and a more unitary structure will develop. Some of the arguments in support of the elimination of class boundaries have already been encountered above. First, it is argued that technical change will result in a greater demand for professional and highly skilled workers and that the proportion of manual or semi-skilled workers will decline. (This does not rule out, of course, an absolute growth in the number of manual workers.) Secondly, say Soviet theorists, the general cultural and educational level of the population as a whole will increase. The position of all workers will improve and become more alike as facilities such as education and consumer goods become widely available. The equalisation of 'consumption' will progressively counterbalance the distinctions associated with different kinds of work. Finally, from this viewpoint the significance of differences in income between strata will be eliminated, partly by the increasing provision of 'free goods' (meals and transport) for all citizens and partly by a reduction of wage differentials themselves. In support of these claims it is pointed out that a general narrowing of basic pay differentials and a greater equalisation of earnings have taken place. (Wage levels are discussed in more detail on pp. 55–62).

But such views should be regarded with caution. Even in 1980 15 per cent of the population were still members of collective farms, and it will take a very long time for conditions in the countryside to approximate to those in the towns. Moreover, as we shall see later on in this book, equal money incomes of social strata are by no means accompanied by identical 'consumption' patterns either of commodities or of educational opportunities. Another criticism of the Soviet notion of *sblizhenie* (drawing together) is that it is not equivalent to the communist idea of the elimination of the distinction between manual and non-manual work. Soviet sociologists recognise that both physical and intellectual work will be necessary for a considerable time to come.

One way of bringing together manual and non-manual labour, which is sometimes suggested in the USSR, is participation in different kinds of work by the same individual. This viewpoint is based on Marx's prognostication that in communist society there would be no division of labour:

> In communist society where nobody has one exclusive sphere of activity but each can become accomplished in any branch he wishes, society regulates the general production and thus makes it possible for me to do one thing today and another tomorrow, to hunt in the morning, fish in the afternoon, rear cattle in the evening, criticize after dinner, just as I have a mind, without ever becoming hunter, fisherman, shepherd or critic. (Marx and Engels, 1965, p. 45)

In the Soviet Union this might be put into practice, as suggested by Elmeev and his colleagues, by a person being both an engineering fitter and teaching history at school (1965, p. 46). At present this possibility is not seriously discussed in the USSR.

It is also sometimes suggested in the Soviet Union that social differences associated with occupations will be diminished with the development of automation. With the growing technical complexity of machinery and the work process it is said that workers will have to be trained in both manual and mental skills to perform a certain task. Hence from this viewpoint, the supervisor of an automated production line must understand, say, electrical engineering and be able to perform skilled manual tasks to keep his line going. He is both a manual and a non-manual worker and in this way manual and mental labour is merged. This process, it is argued, is accompanied by the gradual abolition of manual jobs (road sweepers, machine operators). But in my view this theory does not remove the distinctions which arise between different kinds of work. Not all occupations will be affected by automation and it is doubtful whether all jobs will, in fact, involve both mental and manual labour. For instance, what kind of manual work will be performed by a teacher of sociology? It is also possible that automation may create an even more specialised and stratified division of labour than before (Blumberg, 1968, pp. 53–64) and with the 'deskilling' of many crafts. It is probably to be expected that with the further development of industrial society, the general standards of education will rise as they have done in the past. Again, the development of technology will mean that a higher proportion of the workforce will be 'specialists' and some Soviet sociologists have considerable confidence that the general rise in educational standards will reduce the gap between manual and non-manual workers. But in so far as this tendency is true, there is nothing especially 'communist' about it – it is also characteristic of advanced industrial capitalist societies.

Further difficulties arise over those posts which are concerned with control over production or over other men. In a modern complex industrial society someone must take decisions, and many persons become specialised in administration. Here Soviet theorists do not advocate workers' management or the abolition of conventional administration which would involve a process of genuine 'collective decision-making'. Rather they see opportunities for workers to participate in and 'to control' (in the sense of 'to check' rather than to exercise rights of direction over) the administration through commissions and voluntary organisations (such as trade unions). A more fundamental way in which 'directing roles' are to diminish is through the 'withering away' of the state, that is by an increase in the number of part-time and voluntary participants in the administrative apparatus. This means that the trade unions, for example, will take over greater responsibility for labour discipline, that the Communist Party will exercise influence in industrial problems and that the voluntary militia (*druzhiniki*) will maintain law and public order. (See details in Friedgut, 1979.) In these processes the power of men in executive jobs may be reduced.

As evidence of their progress, Soviet sociologists point out that the number of leaders (*rukovoditeli*) in government administration declined by 14 per cent between 1959 and 1970. But even if this decrease is not explained by changes in the span of control – giving fewer men more power – there were still 123,000 leaders in administration, and the number of directors of industrial enterprises has risen between the two dates by 141 per cent to reach a total of 957,800 in 1970. In addition there are over 119,000 leaders in Party, trade-union and other organisations. These numbers illustrate that the USSR is far from being a society where the number of people who tell others what to do is on the decline.

Social Divisions

In the light of the foregoing data presented on the Soviet notion of the construction of a classless society some critical comments are in order. It seems to me that the really significant difference in the system of social stratification compared to Western industrial societies is the absence of a private propertied class possessing great concentrations of wealth. Otherwise, the USSR is not dramatically unlike Western industrial societies.

One may take issue with the notion that the unequal distribution of rewards is the outcome of the 'law of distribution according to work', as Shkaratan (see above, p. 46) puts it. While some critical Marxists in the West go too far in denying the relevance of skill to earnings, it must be pointed out that the value to society of different types of work has an important social dimension – values mediate between the division of labour and the distribution of rewards. Such values are not only shaped by the political élites (as asserted by critics of the USSR) but also by traditional and deep-seated beliefs about what constitutes a fair and just wage for one person in relation to others. In addition, as in the West, the market plays its hand. Though there are exceptions, workers who have skills requiring training and education and who are in short supply tend to receive a greater financial reward than those who have little or no skill. It would, therefore, seem to be true that the USSR is entering an epoch of classlessness only if one defines class in terms of private individual ownership of productive means. For the rising level of skill and education associated with advanced industrialisation would appear to be creating a system of social inequality which, save for its ownership-class component, is very similar to, if narrower than, that of Western capitalist states. Literacy is universal and an increasingly large, but relatively privileged, part of the population is receiving higher education. The proportion of unskilled jobs is falling and that of highly skilled categories is rising but both groups are likely to persist in the near future. Finally, even though the wage differential previously enjoyed by 'white-collar' workers is gradually giving way to greater equality of income (see pp. 55–6) differential incomes are very much part of the Soviet social structure. Even in the Soviet view of the foreseeable future, it would appear that though social differences are planned to decline, the structure of social inequality is to remain.

In this chapter we have considered the Soviet view of the building of communism. The social differences which have been described might be considered rather superficial ones ignoring many dimensions of social stratification which are important in the eyes of Western critics. Are there any statuses to which individuals defer? Does sex or nationality provide a basis of social inequality? Are there strata within the Soviet system (such as groups of bureaucrats or intellectuals) which dominate, rather than co-operate, with the others? In the next chapters we shall turn to consider these aspects of social stratification as well as other forms of inequality.

3 Social Inequality: Hierarchy and Privilege

While Marxists hold that class position is the central determinant of the system of inequality and social stratification, many, probably most, modern sociologists view stratification as being multidimensional. The clearest and best-known statement of this approach to stratification is that of Parsons: 'Social stratification is . . . the differential ranking of the human individuals who compose a given social system and their treatment as superior and inferior relative to one another in certain socially important respects' (1954, p. 69). Parsons goes on to assert that differential ranking is a 'really fundamental phenomenon of social systems'. In this concept of stratification many social roles and activities may be the bases of evaluation. As Barber has put it:

> What one's job is, how handsomely one dresses, how much one knows, how well one plays games, how good a friend one is, how one practises religion, all these and a multitude of other social roles and activities are potentially bases of evaluation that may be applied to the members of a society in order to determine their relative position in the system of stratification. (1957, pp. 19–20)

In this chapter we shall describe some of the chief ways in which people are differentiated from each other. We shall consider the distribution of income, occupational prestige and the extent to which these and other bases of differentiation such as, for example, those of sex and ethnic origin, correlate with social stratification.

INCOME DIFFERENTIALS

Income is taken by modern sociologists to be an important index of social standing though categories defined by income statistics

54

in themselves may not correspond to social groups, to a style of life or to political privilege. Politicians, for instance, might have little popular prestige, a fairly high income, but supreme political power. Bearing this caveat in mind, income is nevertheless a most important determinant of a person's life chances. Also the distribution of income may indicate the way certain social groups apportion the social surplus of a society. Many egalitarian thinkers regard an equal distribution of income to be an essential characteristic of a just society. Others (and including Soviet writers) argue that wage differences are necessary in modern society to reward achievement and innovation and to ensure that the most suitable persons are allocated to various roles. From this viewpoint, a hierarchy of styles of life, of differential income and consumption patterns, provides a stimulus to achievement which is an integral part of the system of modern production. Hence the legitimacy of income inequality in Soviet-type societies is defended by their spokesmen in similar terms to those defending differentials under capitalism.

We have seen that after 1917 the social hierarchy in Russia was severely disrupted and that wage differentials were reduced as part of this process but were then widened again under Stalin's regime. Since the 1950s differentials have again narrowed. Available Soviet statistics on the levels of earned income are not very comprehensive. 'Average wages' for various groups of industries are published in the annual statistical handbook and these data may be supplemented by other fragments of information on specific kinds of jobs. The official minimum wage in 1981 was 70 roubles per month and the average money wage in 1980 was 168·9 roubles (these include manual and non-manual workers but exclude collective farmers). Data are also published for separate industries: in building the average wage in 1980 was 202 roubles; on state farms 149 roubles; in transport 200 roubles (sailors got 232); in communications 146 roubles; in education 136 roubles; in science 179 roubles; and in administration (offices of government, trade unions, etc.) 156 roubles (*Vestnik statistiki*, 1981, no. 8, p. 78).

If we consider data on the distribution of income in industry, there has been a general upgrading of manual workers' pay and a tendency towards equalisation. Taking manual workers' pay as

100, in 1932 the index of engineers and technicians was 263 and clerical employees 150; by 1960 the ratios were (workers equal 100), engineers and technicians 151, clerical employees 82, and by 1979 the ratios had fallen to 116 and 79 respectively (Tsentral'noe, 1980, p. 394). In this respect, of course, in Britain also the differences between lower-white-collar workers and manual workers have also been reduced (see Bain, 1970, pp. 65–7; Lockwood, 1958, p. 21; Parkin, 1979, pp. 79–80). Hans Aage (1981, p. 18) has compared earnings for various occupations in the USSR and other countries. Taking a skilled worker's income at 100 in each country he has calculated the following relativities for the USSR (UK comparisons are in brackets): unskilled worker 82 (73), engineer 122 (130), teacher 61 (116), physician 89 (161) and clerk 50 (80) – engineers and doctors were relatively even better off in Denmark with ratios of 182 and 195 over the Danish skilled worker's wage. However, it would be misleading to imply that skilled manual workers have a higher income or standard of living than non-manuals. Though *individual* wages may be higher, we must take into account the family situation (the number of dependants and the earnings of spouses). When this is done, non-manuals (including teachers, doctors and scientists, not shown above) come to the top and manuals are below them (see Gordon and Klopov, 1973, p. 42).

In addition to money income is payment in kind or transfers. 'Transfers' involved in social security and government provision apply to the whole population. McAuley estimates that in 1974 just under 20 per cent of the income of state employees, and under 10 per cent of collective-farmers' income was derived from transfer payments. In money terms, expenditure per capita came to 330·8 roubles in 1974: in percentage terms this was divided as follows: holiday pay 14, pensions 26·6, allowances 8·8, stipends 2·5, education 26·8, medical care 14·5, social security 1·1, housing subsidy 5·8 (McAuley, 1979, pp. 35, 262; see further below, pp. 59–60). In addition are other subsidies, particularly on food and other commodities.

The lowest paid are collective farmers. But even here the gap is closing. By the end of the 1960s collective-farmers' total per capita income was from 78 to 85 per cent of that of state employees; between 1970 and 1974, the personal income of state employees rose 4·23 per cent and that of collective farmers 4·68 per cent (McAuley, 1979, pp. 306, 309).

These figures give averages for rather general groups but tell us little about the range of incomes. On the basis of Soviet sources which list wage rates (not actual earnings) we confirm the trend to equalisation. Tables 3.1 and 3.2 show the monthly salaries of directors, by importance of enterprises (I–VII) and the wage scales of different grades of workers. Both tables show an equalising tendency between 1960 and 1975. Other calculations have been cited by Ellman which show that the decile ratio of earnings for all workers and employees fell from 7·24 in 1946 to 2·83 in 1968 and then rose to 3·35 in 1976. (The decile ratio is that of the highest in the bottom 90 per cent of earnings to the highest earnings in the bottom 10 per cent; Ellman, 1980, p. 670). Major inadequacies of such data are that they ignore other forms of income (bonuses and payments in kind) and they also leave out of consideration those who are not in the workforce (e.g. family dependants). We therefore have to turn to discuss rather random sources on individual incomes.

Matthews (1978, pp. 21–7) has provided the clearest picture of élite privileges in the USSR. Based mainly on Jewish *émigré* reports, he points out that in early 1970s when the average monthly wage was 130 roubles, a Party First Secretary received 900 roubles per month (plus payments in kind), a member of a Republican Council of Ministers received 430 roubles (basic) plus 195 roubles in extras (total 625), other salaries included a manager in the coal industry 656 roubles which tallies with an estimate of 450–600 roubles for the directors of a large industrial enterprise given by Yanowitch (1977, p. 39), a Marshal of the USSR – 2,000 roubles, a top ballet dancer 900 to 1,200 roubles per month. Taking a cut-off point of 500 roubles per month, Matthews estimates that the privileged élite numbers 227,000 – about 0·2 per cent of the labour force: Party and state officials are the largest part of the élite (pp. 30–3). In addition to such income inequalities are privileges in kind enjoyed by the élite groups: these include access to 'special shops' which stock goods in short supply, dining rooms at the place of work, rights to transport (cars), special medical facilities, holiday and travel privileges. There can be no doubt that there is a privileged élite in consumption terms earning (in money terms) about five times the average wage and receiving important benefits in kind. It would, however, be biased to ignore the equalising tendencies described earlier in this chapter and it would also be inaccurate to equate consumption privileges in the USSR with those under capitalism. Matthews points out that even when estimates of other benefits are added to the money income of the privileged, the total comes to from five to eight times the average Soviet wage; on his own calculations the income of the corresponding American élite is in the order of twelve times the average American wage. Also Matthews focuses on the American occupational élite and minimises the very large unearned incomes of

Table 3.1 *Salary Structure in Soviet Machinery Industry, 1960 and 1975 (Administrative Salaries)*

Director of Enterprise	Monthly Salary in Roubles by Enterprise Group						
	I	II	III	IV	V	VI	VII
1960	300–30	250–300	220–60	200–30	160–200	150–70	100–40
1975	300–30	250–300	220–60	220–30	190–200	180–90	150–70

Source: Chapman (1979, p. 157).

Table 3.2 *Wage Scales in Machinery and Several other Industries for Manual Workers*

	Grade	I	II	III	IV	V	VI
1960		1·0	1·13	1·29	1·48	1·72	2·00
1975		1·0	1·09	1·20	1·33	1·50	1·71

Source: Chapman (1979, p. 153).

persons derived from massive corporate wealth. As Lenski (1966, p. 27) has pointed out, the very rich in the USA have an income ratio of 7,000:1 between highest and average. Wiles and Markowski conclude, following a comprehensive comparative review of incomes under state socialism and capitalism: 'capitalism produces extremely rich people with a great deal of capital, and this is the most striking difference between [income distribution under communism and capitalism]' (1971, p. 344).

In socialist states the possibilities of enjoying very large incomes are circumscribed by the absence of a leisure class lifestyle and industries catering for the privileged groups – as Matthews points out, the real living standard of the Soviet privileged élite approximates to that of the average living standard in the USA in the 1970s (1978, p. 176). Indeed, the description of the lifestyle of the typical member of the Soviet privileged élite puts it in a quite different category from the privileges of feudal lords, contemporary top capitalists and even the British monarchy. The value system in socialist states does not sanctify such consumption and it can only be enjoyed furtively.

It is difficult to determine which social groups benefit from transfer payments. The highest rate of income tax is 13 per cent (in addition all childless wage earners pay a tax of 6 per cent of earnings) and the tax system therefore is not very progressive, compared to Western states. Very few Soviet studies are available showing which social groups benefit most from social services and government provision. McAuley (1979, pp. 90–8) has commented that between 1956 and 1964 the rouble value of cash receipts from public funds 'has tended to increase with per capita income' (pp. 96–7). One reason for this is that many payments are income-related. Rather more progressive in incidence is that of non-cash income: in one study (for the 1960s) this fell from 9·7 roubles per month for those with incomes under 25 roubles to 4·8 roubles for those having over 70 roubles. Subsidies on food are of obvious benefit to the poor, and the system has also in general, abolished the degradation associated with structural unemployment. But in the case of housing (see below, pp. 63–4) and in education, benefits probably increase with income. It certainly is the case that Soviet social-security programmes still leave many people in poverty. Pensions are linked to level of wages, a low-paid worker will be in great difficulty if he has not completed the full qualifying period of twenty years (for men) or fifteen years (for women). (One Western writer has estimated that in 1978 the average pension paid in the USSR was 32 per cent of the gross monthly wage: Porket, 1981.) Also dependants (if they have not been in employment) will receive only 10 per cent of the pension (or 15 per cent for two or more). Hence for the aged, disabled, single-parent families, there are many gaps in the system of social security which leave a minority in considerable poverty (see further, George and Manning, 1980, pp. 44–63). The principle of reward according to one's work strongly influences the level of social-security payments and obscures the needs of many deserving groups. Taking the per capita poverty line at 50 roubles per month, McAuley has estimated that some 40 per cent of the Soviet population were below this level in the late 1960s (1977, p. 234).

Kemeny's study of poverty in Hungary showed that about a third of the Hungarian population was living below the subsistence minimum in 1968 and he calculates that by 1973 a fifth of the population was 'poor' and one-tenth 'very poor' (1979, pp. 248–9). Of the 'very poor' group, 70 per cent of the heads of households were employed, while 30 per cent were living on pensions or social security. Of the employed, 65 per cent of the heads of households were industrial workers and the balance was made up of agricultural labourers (p. 249). The 'very poor' tended to be in large families, with the mother doing no work or only casual labour. Kemeny calculates that in 1973, of families with four or more children, 83 per cent were 'poor' and 63 per cent 'very poor' (p. 252).

Western observers often take a very high threshold for not being in poverty: it is often as high as 40 per cent of the average wage, whereas the poverty line in the West is usually estimated at 20 per cent of average earnings. Estimates are only rough indices and not authoritative measures of individual needs. The raising of the minimum wage, the improvement of the earnings of collective farmers and the rise in child allowances, have certainly made this group smaller by the early 1980s. While I concur with George and Manning that 'the dominant ideology of the USSR provides a more secure environment for the growth of social policy' (1980, p. 169) it is also true that 'socialist social policies are no more vertically redistributive than welfarist social policies' (p. 172).

While Soviet data on income distribution are not very adequate much better statistics are available for other Eastern European societies. In Poland wage differentials have followed a similar general pattern through time as in the Soviet Union. This is not surprising, of course, for after the Second World War the USSR was used as a model for the state-socialist societies of Eastern Europe. In the immediate postwar period in Poland there occurred a reduction in the level of differentials compared to prewar Poland. One calculation has shown that in 1937 non-manual workers received three times as much as manual workers whereas their advantage was only 9 per cent greater in 1960. Comparing the range of incomes (highest and lowest) Wesolowski (1966) estimates that this has fallen from 200:1 in prewar Poland to 10:1 in the 1960s. The distribution of incomes between manual and non-manual workers in 1963 is shown in Table 3.3. While there are eight times as many manual workers as non-manual workers in the very lowest category, and one and a half times as many non-manuals as manuals in the top group, it can be seen that the majority of each falls in the range of 1,201–2,500 zlotys. Of course, the very high incomes, well over 3,000 zlotys which are not defined here in detail, are probably to be found among the highest non-manual strata.

Table 3.3 *Polish Gross Monthly Earnings according to Wage Groups (1963)*

Wage group (zlotys)	Manual (percentage)		Non-manual (percentage)	
701–800	10·7		1·3	
801–1,000	7·2		5·4	
1,001–1,200	8·7		9·1	59·2
1,201–1,500	15·6		17·1	
1,501–2,000	24·7		26·3	
2,001–2,500	15·9		16·3	
2,501–3,000	8·5	33·1	10·4	
over 3,000	8·7		14·1	

Source: Cited by Wesolowski (1966, p. 27).

We may confidently generalise that it seems to be a general pattern in state-socialist societies that the period immediately following the nationalisation of property and the seizure of political power is characterised by income equalisation. Later, with the consolidation of power by the new élites, greater differentials are introduced. In the USSR Stalin, by virtue of his administrative control, implemented such changes whereas in Eastern Europe it is the self-styled anti-Stalinists who have called for greater reliance on market mechanisms, financial incentives and the abolition of the 'damaging levelling of wages'. (Many economists in Czechoslovakia associated with the reform movement of Dubcek have argued that wage equality has had a most deleterious effect on the development and growth of the economy: Müller, 1969, pp. 48–9; Sik, 1967, pp. 203–4; Machonin, 1969, p. 158.)

The suppression of independent trade unions has also restricted the articulation of interests of groups of workers seeking to assert their rights to higher income. It seems unlikely that the 'free trade-union' movement in Poland which began in the 1980s would have led to policies which were vertically redistributive, indeed, it may well be that by securing a high share for wages, the proportion spent on social-security provision would have fallen.

CONSUMPTION PATTERNS

The extent of income differences may be illustrated by research carried out in Hungary which provides data on patterns of consumption as well as income (Hungarian Central Statistical Office, 1967; a survey of 1,500 households carried out in 1963). The Hungarian research shows not only that wage income is differentiated, but also that it is spent on different things thereby giving rise to differing 'styles of living'.

> In the groups in a more advantageous situation, and especially with a higher education, there is a strong trend toward the realisation of a way of life which they consider more cultured . . . The total yearly expense of education and entertainment increases from 86 forints in the group of agricultural cooperative members to 486 forints in the group of leading officials, intellectuals . . . At the same time, there is only a 60 per cent difference in the value of total consumption. (p. 79)

The top group spent 3·5 times more than average on

newspapers, 2·5 more on the cinema, 33 times more on books and 8 times as much on going to the theatre. The authors point out that the better educated strata not only have a 'more cultural manner of life' but eat better kinds of food, spend more on holidays and utilise more household appliances (washing machines, refrigerators, etc.).

Those with more income and better education also have a greater variety of consumption goods, which 'in certain cases reflect the demand for goods which are symbols of the social position' (p. 80). Higher professional occupation groups consume 5·5 times more coffee than unskilled operatives. They eat less beans, cabbage and bread but more mushrooms, asparagus and rolls. The top group spends 54 forints per capita per annum on cosmetics, whereas the unskilled operatives only spend 19 forints. On domestic help and laundry, the upper professional groups spend 164 forints, other non-manual 83 forints, skilled/semi-skilled 29 forints, unskilled 17 forints, and agricultural co-operative workers only 4 forints. As the sample excluded households with domestic help living in, the actual differences are even greater than shown (p. 81).

The higher social groups also made greater use of the social services. While the health service is free, medicine is not. Leading officials and intellectuals spent 34 forints per capita per annum on medicine, and other non-manual workers, 37 forints: but such spending by skilled/semi-skilled workers fell to 22 forints and by agricultural co-operative workers to 19 forints. Housing is also differentiated by social group: the higher the social status, the better the housing. Some of the chief results of the Hungarian survey are summarised in Table 3.4. It suggests a highly hierarchical social structure with a remarkably high correlation between income, housing and cultural level. Research conducted in Czechoslovakia shows lower but positive correlation between income, prestige and education. Safar *et al.*, following field research involving 13,215 respondents, have shown that 'style of life' is highly correlated with income (0·45), complexity of work (0·54) and education (0·61) (1970, p. 18).

Studies in the Soviet Union point to an equalising tendency in the differences in consumption between various strata. Considering outlays on cultural goods, Kogan points out that in 1940

Table 3.4   *Social Position, Per Capita Income, Housing and Cultural Indexes*

Social strata by occupation of head of household	Per capita income index (average = 100) (A)	Index of housing standards [a] (average = 100) (B)	Index of cultural level [b] (average = 100) (C)
Higher professionals	151	149	193
Average-level experts	125	133	153
Office clerks	117	128	147
Skilled workers	107	109	110
Trained workers	93	91	87
Unskilled workers	81	86	67
Agricultural manual workers	86	79	60

Source: Adapted from Ferge (1966).

[a] Based on size, conveniences and equipment of houses.

[b] Cultural level combines average level of education of family, books, newspapers, radio and TV.

Correlation coefficient columns A/B 0·97

A/C 0·98

B/C 0·99.

Table 3.5   *Index of Cultural Interests of Different Social Groups*

	Manual Workers		'Specialists'		Clerical Employees	
Cinema	1·00	I	1·00	I	1·00	I
Television	0·61	II	0·51	V	0·68	III
Literature	0·56	III	0·85	II	0·58	V
Variety (concert)	0·54	IV	0·47	VI	0·50	VII
Music	0·49	V	0·62	IV	0·52	VI
Circus	0·44	VI	0·32	VII	0·60	IV
Theatre	0·39	VII	0·78	III	0·80	II

Source: Kogan (1977, p. 39).

Survey based on random sample in 1974 of social groups in two districts of Sverdlovsk. Index expressed is proportions of choice for each group, with cinema attendance at 1.

a family of workers in industry would spend on average 17·5 per cent of its income compared to 4·4 per cent of a peasant's. In 1974, however, the comparative figures were 23 per cent and 15·1 per cent (1977, p. 39). Kogan constructs an index of attendance by manual workers, specialists and clerical employees at different kinds of entertainment. Examination of Table 3.5 shows considerable differences in cultural pursuits by the various groups. The cinema is clearly the major leisure interest of all three groups, but attendance at the theatre is second for clerical employees (mainly female), third for 'specialists' and seventh (bottom of their preferences) for manual workers.

We may conclude that while the range of money incomes is narrowed by the political authorities, nevertheless social strata in state-socialist societies are distinguished by differences in income and consumption patterns which are related to the place occupied in the division of labour. Occupation appears to give rise to not only various quantitative differences in consumption, but to qualitative ones as well which manifest themselves in variations in the style and manner of life. The hypothesis that the major 'break' in the stratification system of state-socialist societies lies between skilled and unskilled rather than, as in Western capitalist societies, between manual and non-manual must be treated with some scepticism (Parkin, 1971, p. 147). While a reduction in differentials between non-manual and manual has taken place, this need not entail a 'proletarianisation' of the white-collar worker. As Goldthorpe *et al.* have been at pains to point out in respect of the notion of the 'bourgeoisification' of the English proletariat, even a convergence of certain aspects of the life situation of manual and non-manual workers has not led to the assimilation of the former by the latter (1969, pp. 23–9).

The discussion so far suffers from many defects: the inequalities described are mostly quantitative and the categories used have been devised mainly for statistical and economic purposes. While these deficiencies do not make invalid the inequalities described, they limit the sociological inferences we may wish to make. We do not know, for example, whether these categories are socially meaningful. Are the members of different income groups conscious of being in a status hierarchy, of being a stratum with a distinctive social standing relative to other groups? It is possible that the kinds of inequality described do not flow over into the evaluation of men in the numerous roles they play. It is claimed by many Soviet sociologists that individuals may be differentiated by skill, income and sex, but that a system of social evaluation or honour does not follow from these inequalities. The values of Soviet society, they say, are those of fraternal equality and the leaders of the Communist Party and factory labourers may regard each other as 'comrades' (for a different interpretation see Ossowski, 1963, p. 190). This may not be as fanciful as it may seem at first sight, for many commentators on the American social structure concede its objective inequality but argue that 'its nature as a non deferential society . . . is a quality of the national existence marked by European visitors and observers since the early nineteenth century' (Connor, 1979, p. 316).

OCCUPATIONAL PRESTIGE AND SOCIAL GROUPINGS

Data available on status hierarchy in Soviet society are to be found in a study by Western sociologists of the evaluation of occupational roles in industrial societies. This research considers the prestige given to occupations in the USSR in relation to similar studies in five other advanced countries. The sources of the Soviet data were interviews conducted with 2,146 Soviet displaced persons after the Second World War. The similarities in prestige ratings between the countries were measured by correlation coefficients and the results affecting the USSR and other countries are shown in Table 3.6.

Table 3.6 *Comparisons of Occupational Prestige Ratings in USSR and Other Countries*

	Japan	*UK*	*New Zealand*	*USA*	*Germany*
USSR	0·74	0·83	0·83	0·90	0·90

Source: Inkeles and Rossi (1956, p. 332).

Here we see a remarkable similarity between the rankings. The researchers also analysed the discrepancies in each nation's ratings which account for the absence of a unitary correlation.

The discrepancies in ranking of occupations are shown on Table 3.7.

Table 3.7 *Differences in Occupational Rankings in the USSR and Other Countries*

Rated higher in:	Japan	USA	UK	New Zealand
Rated lower in USSR	Factory manager	Scientist	Farmer	Farmer
	Farmer	Farmer		
Rated lower in:	Japan	USA	UK	New Zealand
Rated higher in USSR	Accountant	Engineer	Worker	Worker
		Worker		

Source: Adapted from Inkeles and Rossi (1956, p. 334).

The table brings out the main differences in the ranking of occupations. From it we may fairly safely make two inferences. First, the lower ranking given to the 'farmer' in the USSR is probably explained both by the inferior status given to the *krestyanin* (peasant) in pre-revolutionary Russia and to his *de facto* underprivilege in Soviet Russia. Secondly, the relatively exalted position of 'the worker' in the Soviet Union is directly attributable to the value system of communism. In the view of its authors, the general implications of this research are that 'there is a relatively invariable hierarchy of prestige associated with the industrial system, even when it is placed in the context of larger social systems which are otherwise differentiated in important respects' (p. 339).

The Soviet data utilised above were based on respondents' views on the 'general desirability' of the occupations. This is not the same as 'popular regard', or personal safety or personal satisfaction. Rossi and Inkeles (1957), using the same respondents have analysed the ratings given to occupations in five dimensions: general desirability, material position, personal satisfaction, safety (from arrest), popular regard. The desirability of occupations was highly correlated to personal satisfaction ($+0 \cdot 898$), and quite highly correlated to popular regard ($+0 \cdot 525$). On the other hand, jobs held high in popular regard were low on material position ($-0\cdot180$): hence a doctor who was ranked first in popular regard was seventh in material position. Material position and safety were very negatively correlated ($-0\cdot818$): the 'safest' occupation was believed to be 'rank-and-file worker', but its material position was bottom but one; on the other hand, a factory manager was ranked second in material position but was at the bottom of the safety scale.

While the above study of Soviet refugees has contributed greatly to our knowledge of stratification in the Soviet Union it refers to a period before 1941 and unfortunately the study of status and occupational prestige has not been carried out in the Soviet Union. Some Soviet sociologists have been concerned with specifying just how the 'social division of labour' affects various occupational positions and others have investigated in some detail the preferability of various occupations – especially in the eyes of school-leavers. Shkaratan and Rukavishnikov (1977) have attempted to define the stratification of various groups making up the working class in the USSR. They have constructed an 'index of the character of work' which ranks seventy-five different occupations. This is derived from points given to each occupation for its executive and organisational functions, its complexity and mental strain, its degree of independence in the work situation and the complexity of the task (see ibid., pp. 63–5). The top occupations (i.e. the ones with the highest score) were the director and chief engineer of an industrial enterprise, the director of a scientific research institute, the head of a (scientific) laboratory, the head of the division of the local food industry, the chief medical consultant (*vrach*); at the bottom of the list came medical orderly, doorkeeper, porter, unskilled and semi-skilled manual workers and dockers (*gruzchik*). In summary, the scale rose from unskilled manual to professional posts. Vodzinskaya (1973) asked secondary school pupils in Leningrad to rank forty occupations in terms of their creativity, prestige and 'overall attractiveness'. The results are reproduced in Table 3.8. (For other Soviet studies of this topic see Lane and O'Dell, 1978, pp. 73–7.)

Table 3.8 *Distribution of Occupations on the Scales of Attractiveness (Preferred Selection) (S), Creativity (C) and Social Prestige (P) According to the Evaluations of Boy and Girl Graduates of Leningrad's Secondary Schools (N = 124)*

			Rank			
Occupation		Boys			Girls	
	S	C	P	S	C	P
(1) Physicist	1	1	3	2	2	1
(2) Mathematician	2	4	1	6	4	2
(3) Radio engineer	3	2	6	5	9	14
(4) Radio technician	4	5	10	9	13	17
(5) Scientific worker	5	3	2	3	3	3
(6) Pilot	6	14	5	4	16	4
(7) Chemical engineer	7	7	8	10	10	9
(8) Mechanical engineer	8	10	12	14	15	16
(9) Geologist	9	11	11	7	6	8
(10) Physician	10	8	7	1	7	5
(11) Higher-education teacher	11	12	9	12	11	7
(12) Philosopher	12	9	13	18	5	11
(13) Construction engineer	13	13	15	12	12	16
(14) Metallurgical engineer	14	16	14	15	17	13
(15) Philologist	15	15	17	11	8	12
(16) Driver	16	31	27	20	27	25
(17) Worker in literature and art	17	6	4	8	1	6
(18) Locksmith	18	20	22	35	30	33
(19) Shipbuilder	19	16	20	17	20	21
(20) Automatic equipment setter	20	19	21	27	30	30
(21) Automatic equipment operator	21	21	24	24	29	28
(22) Mechanic	22	21	25	30	30	32
(23) Secondary-school teacher	23	18	16	13	14	10
(24) Steel founder	24	26	18	30	28	23
(25) Chemical worker	25	29	31	28	32	26
(26) Lathe operator	26	30	26	29	31	29
(27) Railroad worker	27	33	32	28	35	30
(28) Agronomist	28	21	30	27	19	20
(29) Installation worker in construction	29	30	31	28	33	31
(30) Tractor operator, combine operator	30	32	31	37	32	30
(31) Culture and education worker	31	29	28	21	20	24
(32) Cook, waiter	32	32	36	32	24	33
(33) Kindergarten teacher	33	28	23	20	18	19
(34) Livestock worker	34	33	34	31	28	36
(35) Housepainter	35	37	37	37	38	37
(36) Field worker	36	36	36	35	29	34

69

(37) Tailor, seamstress	37	27	34	32	23	30
(38) Clerical worker	38	40	40	38	39	39
(39) Housing-maintenance worker	39	38	39	40	40	40
(40) Shop assistant	40	39	35	35	36	38

Source: Vodzinskaya (1973, pp. 169–70).

While Soviet sociologists have only indirectly considered the subjectively held 'status' or 'prestige' of occupations, Polish sociologists have carried out work which is more comparable with Western studies. In a comparative study Sarapata (1966, p. 41) has calculated the correlation between 'Western' and Polish prestige hierarchies: the correlations were, Poland (Warsaw) and England 0·862, Poland (Warsaw) and West Germany 0·879. These statistics must be carefully interpreted. The rankings are restricted to comparable occupations, and some important categories, such as Party Secretary, are excluded from the cross-national calculations. Also the Polish data refer to the metropolis and not to the countryside where more traditional values may persist. Secondly, the 'rankings' may overlook significant differences in social distance and may be too gross in character to show up other socially significant variations. For instance, while the occupations of trained engineer and skilled worker may have similar 'ranks' in two societies, the relative degree of the 'desirability' of their jobs may be very different and the process of interaction between the groups is yet another distinct question.

Table 3.9 shows what people thought of the status of certain occupations in modern Poland as compared with their status in prewar Poland. Workers using their hands, both skilled and unskilled, rose very much in popular esteem whereas non-manual groups (such as merchants and priests) suffered a decline. Thus the impact of nationalisation, of the ideology of state socialism, cannot be dismissed as unimportant: it had a profound effect not only in changing the occupational structure but also on the prestige of some occupations.

Analysing eleven social surveys carried out in Poland between 1958 and 1973, Wesolowski and Slomczynski (1977) found correlation of 0·94 in the mean value of the rank ordering of

Table 3.9 *Respondents' Evaluations of the Change in Status of Selected Occupations (in Percentages)*

Occupation	As compared with the prewar period the status of the occupation is now		
	Higher	The same	Lower
Engineer	39	35	26
Locksmith working for wages	49	21	30
Miner coal-hewer	81	14	5
Unskilled building worker	68	21	11
White-collar worker	24	32	44
Workshop owner	15	25	60
Merchant	9	25	66
Priest	8	25	67

Source: Sarapata (1966, p. 38).

occupational hierarchies. The hierarchy of socio-occupational groups was as follows: professionals, technicians, foremen, skilled workers, office workers, service workers, craftsmen, unskilled workers, farmers, farm labourers (Wesolowski and Slomczynski, 1977, p. 80).

The upshot of these various studies is that the upper-professional occupations, as they are called in the West, stand out as being consistently high in desirability and popular regard. At the other end of the scale are unskilled jobs, both manual and non-manual. Those with the social function of control of life itself (physician) or the understanding and mastery of nature (scientist and engineer) are almost always given wide social recognition and high prestige.

A study which attempts to link up the various measures of inequality to form a comprehensive picture of social stratification in state-socialist society has been conducted by Machonin (1970) in Czechoslovakia. (This survey of 13,215 heads of households, 0·5 per cent sample, was carried out in 1967.) Machonin identified four main groups in which social position was highly crystallised and three subsidiary groups in which there were inconsistent statuses. These are shown on Figure 3.1.

Strata A and B are composed of non-manual groups. The first, making up 4·7 per cent of the sample, has a highly consistent profile. Its members have a secondary or university education, are employed in specialised higher professional positions. Such men have highly cultural leisure pursuits, live in towns, have authority in management and command the highest incomes. The second stratum (B) is constituted of lower-grade, urban white-collar workers with secondary education, a quite high lifestyle and income, and considerable participation in management.

Strata C and D are manual workers. Stratum C is made up of skilled and semi-skilled industrial workers with elementary education. They have an average cultural level of lifestyle and low participation in management. Their average income, however, though below the non-manual groups, is relatively above their scores on other indexes. Stratum D is formed of agricultural workers and semi-skilled and unskilled industrial workers having at most a secondary education, a low income and hardly any participation in management.

The groups with inconsistent statuses are designated by the figures 1, 2 and 3. Group 1 is made up of semi-skilled or skilled manual workers with elementary education employed in unskilled jobs, with a low style of life rating and a very low index of participation in management. The members of this group, however, have a very high income. Group 2 has a profile which nearly reciprocates that of Group 1. It is composed of lower non-manual workers, particularly clerks in large cities, with lower vocational education and fairly high 'style-of-life' rating. It has a low income and a low index of participation in management. Group 3 follows the pattern of Group 1, being constituted of skilled or semi-skilled workers doing semi-skilled work, with abnormally high incomes and a very high rating of leisure activity, though low participation in management (Machonin, 1970, pp. 735–6).

Machonin's work throws some light on the question which was raised earlier (p. 65) of whether a merging of the white-collar and manual strata has taken place. Despite a relative equalisation of incomes, it does not seem to be the case that the distinction between manual and non-manual work has been obliterated. At the top of the social hierarchy (Groups A and B) are two non-manual groups with higher rankings on all dimensions than the

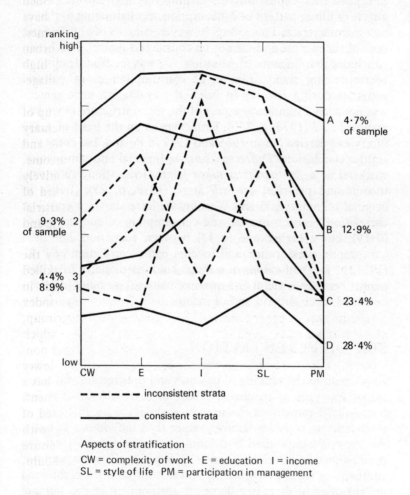

ranking
high

A 4·7%
of sample

9·3% 2
of sample

B 12·9%

4·4% 3
8·9% 1

C 23·4%

D 28·4%

low
CW   E   I   SL   PM

-------- inconsistent strata

———— consistent strata

Aspects of stratification
CW = complexity of work   E = education   I = income
SL = style of life   PM = participation in management

Figure 3.1 *Social strata in Czechoslovakia (1967), based on Machonin
(1970, p. 733).*

bottom two manual groups (C and D). The data from Groups 1
and 2 show that even where industrial workers earn very high
incomes and the unskilled white-collar workers very low, their

'style-of-life' index is inverted. Only in Group 3 is there evidence to suggest that manual workers earning very high incomes adopt a style of life or pattern of consumption approximating to that of non-manual strata. This group, however, consists of only 4·6 per cent of the sample and cannot be considered typical. Machonin concludes that 'income equalisation . . . was far from leading to corresponding standardisation of consumption or of cultural activities during leisure. In brief, the egalitarian arrangement was not such a significant aspect of the social structure as we had assumed . . .' (1970, p. 740). Slomczynski, on the basis of 3,381 interviews carried out in 1965 and 1967 in Poland, has come to a similar conclusion: *'Differences between* [manual and non-manual workers] *at a few variables taken jointly* [education, authority, income and prestige] *are still large'* (1970, p. 25). (Italics in original.) Slomczynski and Wesolowski have shown a very low correlation between income and consumption of cultural goods (0·19), but a higher one (0·43) between education and such consumption. Education and income had a correlation of 0·21 (1974, p. 7). Distinctions of a social kind, particularly lifestyles, persist between manual and non-manual workers quite independently of levels of skill and of income.

SEX DIFFERENTIATION

In addition to the ranking of incomes and prestige are two other important types of inequality: those of sex and ethnicity. Sex inequality is sometimes obscured by sociologists because there is a tendency to consider families rather than individuals as units. As Parsons has pointed out, family status is derived from the occupational role of the husband (1954, p. 80). This has been put another way by Engels when he said that the family was founded on 'the open or disguised domestic enslavement of the woman' (1951, p. 211). The role of the woman in Western societies of today has changed significantly compared with that of the woman in the nineteenth-century family, which Engels had in mind, mainly because the opportunities outside the traditional roles (wife, mother, daughter) have increased. But in Western capitalist countries, even though women enjoy legal equality they are, in fact, largely excluded from certain occupations. In Britain between 1911 and 1966 the proportion of women in the 'employers and proprietors' group rose steadily from 18·8 per cent to 23·7 per cent, but their share of 'managers and administrators' fell from 19·8 per cent to 16·7 per cent; of 'higher professionals' they accounted for 6 per cent and 9·4 per cent (Bain, Bacon and Pimlott, 1972, p. 114).

Parsons has suggested that role specialisation by sex promotes family solidarity and prevents competition between husband and wife. Even when employed outside the home, Parsons asserts that woman's occupations are 'not in direct competition for status with those of men of their own class'. Their employment position differs from men: in England some 30 per cent of those employed are in part-time work; and for those working full-time, wages are 71 per cent of men's for manual labour and 62 per cent for non-manual (data for 1976). This is a general tendency in Western societies (see Swafford, 1978, p. 670). In the USSR in the 1960–74 period, women's wages ranged from 60 to 72 per cent of men's (McAuley, 1981, p. 21). The standards of judgement often applied to women are still related to their personal charm, physical beauty and sexual desirability. Can one say the same about women in state-socialist society?

At first sight, women in the USSR would appear to be more nearly equal to men than is the case in Western capitalist states. Since the early days of the Soviet regime attempts have been made to emancipate women from male domination. Perhaps the best indicators of the changing position of women are their access to higher education and to the occupations traditionally reserved for men. From 1928 to 1935, women's share of the places in institutions of higher education increased from 28 per cent to 38 per cent and by 1941 rose to over 50 per cent. The proportion has remained at 51 per cent since the mid 1970s (Tsentral'noe, 1979, p. 483). This is greater than in Western countries where the share of women in higher educational institutions in total is over 40 per cent (USA 46 per cent, Great Britain 41 per cent, Western Germany 41 per cent). By 1979 women also accounted for 59 per cent of all professional employees (i.e. those with specialist secondary and higher educational qualifications) in the USSR, including 69 per cent of the doctors and 71 per cent of the teachers ('Zhenshchiny v SSSR', 1981, pp. 72–3). It was during the 1930s that women began to enter a wide range of industrial occupations: in 1928 women constituted 24 per cent of the workers in industry as a whole, whereas by 1978 their proportion had risen to 51 per cent (Tsentral'noe, 1979, p. 369).

The Soviet Union has one of the highest participation rates of women (86 per cent) in paid full-time employment. (In Western Germany only 35 per cent and in Britain 43 per cent of women are in paid work. Of these, in Britain 41 per cent and in Germany 28 per cent work only part-time; Oakley, 1981, p. 160.) Interruption of work is also very low: it fell from $12 \cdot 3$ years in 1960 to $3 \cdot 6$ years in 1970 (Pankratova and Yankova, 1978, p. 20). At the time of the 1897 census 55 per cent of all employed women were in domestic service, 25 per cent in agriculture, 13 per cent in industry and building and only 4 per cent in the health and educational services. By 1974, 32 per cent of employed women were in industry and 21 per cent in health and education (*Zhenshchiny*, 1975, p. 30).

Despite these real advances, women still suffer some discrimination when one investigates their participation in work. Women not only tend to be concentrated in certain industries, but their levels of skill and responsibility (see below) are lower than men's. In 1975 women accounted for just over 25 per cent of the entrants to trade schools where they were mainly concentrated in apparatus-building, radio and textiles (Lane and O'Dell, 1978, pp. 116–17). There is a labelling of jobs, some being suitable to 'women's work' – the caring professions, domestic, retail trade, textiles. Though these figures show occupational gender segregation in many trades, the USSR is still ahead of Western countries in this respect: in 1978 in Great Britain, for example, only $0 \cdot 007$ of 1 per cent of craftsmen in the whole of the mechanical engineering industry were women and the proportion of apprentices in that industry was even slightly lower than the previous figure (figures calculated from HMSO, 1980, section VI). Hence, it might well be argued that if Soviet trade schools admit women to 714 out of 1,100 occupations, this is comparatively mild discrimination compared to Great Britain (cf. Lapidus, 1980, p. 4). (In the EEC in 1980 there were twenty-six professions for which governments had refused to pass legislation giving women equal opportunity; *Guardian*, 20 December 1980). One study of skill levels showed that in the USSR in the highest level were 5 per cent of the women, whereas 19 per cent of the men were in this group; at the other extreme, in the lowest skill level, 11 per cent of the workers were female and 9 per cent were men (Karapetyan, 1968; cited by Swafford, 1978, p. 665).

In the non-European areas of the country, the employment of women increased very markedly under the Soviet regime – eight times in Central Asia and Kazakhstan and nearly five times in Transcaucasia. Even so, some inequalities persist: the female participation rate in the economy is lower: compared to 51 per cent of the workforce in the USSR in 1980, it was 42 per cent in Uzbekistan, 43 per cent in Azerbaydzhan and fell to 41 per cent in Turkmenistan ('Zhenshchiny v SSSR', 1981, p. 71). The proportion of women in higher education is also somewhat lower than for the non-Europeans: in 1970 for Russians the index of women with higher and secondary education was 487 (per 1,000 of women aged over 10 years) whereas it fell to 378 for Turkmens and 332 for Kazakhs (*Zhenshchiny*, 1975, p. 64). By 1979, for the employed population, the index (per 1,000) for women with higher, incomplete higher and specialist secondary education was 207 in the Russia Republic; in Turkmenistan it was 137 and 188 in Kazakhstan. (These data, of course, include women of all nationalities in these republics; *Vestnik statistiki*, no. 2, 1981, pp. 64–77.) These figures, it should be borne in mind, are grossly superior participation rates to all other Central Asian countries. It need hardly be added that traditional practices such as polygyny, the bride price and female circumcision have been legally proscribed.

There can be no doubt then that the impact of Soviet communism has had important effects in changing the social structure by opening up opportunities for women not only in higher education and the professional occupations but also in the middle range of skills previously monopolised by men.

A priori, the higher occupational status of Soviet women in general would imply different relations between the sexes, with the possibility of greater competition between men and women in those spheres of life which play a major role in determining status. But in fact the standards of judgement are not independent of sex. Even though the cruder exploitation of women in the form of sexually titillating advertising, beauty competitions and wide-scale prostitution is strictly banned, milder forms of sex differentiation persist in forms of dress and hairstyle and in the use of cosmetics, and imply the evaluation of women on criteria outside the occupational status-giving sphere.

In many other ways women's inequality persists. It is still the rule that men take the initiative in the relationships between the sexes: the choosing of partners in Soviet dance halls is usually a male prerogative, overtures for sexual intercourse generally originate from the male. Though women's sexual enjoyment has been furthered because the legal and quite widespread practice of abortion has reduced the fear of unwanted children, the availability of birth-control pills varies between socialist states. In Hungary they are widely available, but can only be obtained with great difficulty in the USSR (comparative data on birth control, see Jancar, 1978, pp. 69–73). It is very difficult to procure data on sexual satisfaction and on whether the high proportion of women in paid employment leads to psychological stress or whether it opens up greater opportunities for social contacts. In the USSR there is no public discussion, let alone endorsement, of individual sexuality and liberation as advocated in the West by writers such as Reich, and the topics portrayed in the Yugoslav film *WR – Mysteries of the Orgasm* are taboo. One study of female orgasms conducted in the German Democratic Republic reports that 27 per cent of women experience orgasm during intercourse 'nearly every time', 17 per cent 'mostly', 12 per cent 'often', 19 per cent 'casually', 16 per cent 'rarely' and 9 per cent 'never' (Schnabl, 1978, p. 15; cited by Gransow, 1980, p. 11). A study in Bulgaria found that 71 per cent of a sample of women regarded sexual intercourse as being 'meaningful', if 'backed up by love'; only a fifth of the male sample shared this view and the majority sought sexual intercourse as a form of personal gratification (*Times Higher Educational Supplement*, 20 February 1981).

In the USSR family break-up as measured by the divorce rate is fairly high: in 1979 it was 3·6 per 1,000 of the population; in

1979 the ratio of divorces to marriages was 36:109. In the non-European parts of the USSR the divorce rate is approximately 40 per cent of the national average (1·4 in Uzbekistan, and Tadzhikistan and 1·7 in Kirgiziya). But it is rising: in Uzbekistan from 1·1 per 1,000 in 1970 to 1·4 in 1978. It is also noteworthy that here nearly two-fifths of the divorces are initiated by the wife, and urban women do so more frequently than rural (Tashtemirov, 1981, p. 115). These data indicate a fairly high level of independence on the part of women, though a lower yet growing level of emancipation among the central Asian nationalities.

The family name may legally be adopted from either spouse but in practice it is taken from the male side. But the emancipation of women has not yet led to a significant lightening of her domestic burdens and Soviet studies of the utilisation of time have shown that women still bear the brunt of food preparation and domestic cleaning. A survey in Gorki showed that women spent 40·34 hours per week on housework and shopping, etc., whereas the figure for men was 24·45 (Osipov and Frolov, 1966, p. 238). Another study showed that of women with children, 30·45 hours per week were spent on household work, compared to 12·10 hours for a comparable group of men; unmarried women were engaged in housework for 17·40 hours compared to 5·40 hours for unmarried men (Gruzdeva, 1975, p. 96). There is often an assumption in state-socialist societies that 'childcare and cooking are . . . woman's "natural" sphere of activity and . . . that . . . this work [is] women's "natural duty" ' (Molyneux, n.d., p. 20). The amount of free time available to women is about half of that of men and empirical studies of job advancement show that for men to have children does not hinder their chances of a better job; for women, however, the arrival of children does have a negative effect on career advancement (Lukina, 1979, pp. 130–1).

It is only when one considers authority roles that discrimination becomes obvious. In medicine, whereas women make up 69 per cent of the physicians, the number of chief doctors is 53 per cent; and in education, whereas women teachers are some 70 per cent of the total, their numbers fall to 37 per cent of the heads of eight-year schools and to 32 per cent of middle schools, though for primary schools 80 per cent of heads are female ('Zhenshchiny v SSSR', 1981, pp. 72–3).

Women also have less representation among the various élites. Postgraduate women students, for instance, made up only 28 per cent of the total postgraduate students (candidate of sciences) in 1979 and they constituted 14 per cent of the doctors of science; in 1970 women accounted for 10 per cent of the academic élite (Academicians, corresponding members of the Academy and professors). In 1973 only 9 per cent of directors of enterprises, 16 per cent of all heads (and deputies) of workshops and 24 per cent of foremen were female (*Zhenshchiny v SSSR*, 1975, p. 80). Women tend to be occupied less in jobs requiring a directional role over men and more in tasks which require specialised knowledge of things. In 1973, 78 per cent of technicians were female, as were 86 per cent of engineer economists, planners and statisticians.

In politics, whereas women make up 50 per cent of deputies in local government, they account for a third of the members of the Supreme Soviet ('Zhenshchiny v SSSR', 1981, p. 69). In a study of women's participation in elected offices of the government, Maher (1980, p. 189) found that in the period 1958–74 women made up 9·5 per cent of the membership of the Praesidium and were 17·8 per cent of deputies in named offices; they tended to be re-elected less frequently than men. In 1981 women made up 26 per cent of Party members (24·3 per cent in 1976). To the Party Congress in 1981 they constituted 26·6 per cent of the delegates, but only 3 per cent of the voting members of the Central Committee. Furthermore, in 1976, not one of the seventy-two regional Party secretaries was female, though 31 per cent of the local secretaries were; and not one of the 1981 Politburo is female. Of the top hundred leading Soviet officials (see definition of this group below, pp. 92–3) not one is a woman, and in the 1981 Council of Ministers not one woman is included. (For republican data on women in the Party, see Harasymiw, 1980.) The Council of Ministers includes the top industrialists and if a comparison be made with the West, it should include the heads of the top monopolies such as ICI, Ford, BP, etc.

Thus despite the attempts by the Communists to give equality to women, some forms of gender inequality in the USSR have persisted. It would be superficial to attribute such inequality just to the policy of the Communist rulers. The inequality of woman has origins going back to the evolution of man, and beliefs about the inherent differences between sexes and differential expectations of them are passed on unconsciously during the period of childhood socialisation. There are also important biological differences between man and woman. Political changes cannot alter the biological fact that women bear children, and this creates a strong nexus between mother and child. Laws ignoring biological inequality may not enhance her equality but in the absence of comprehensive services are likely to increase her possible exploitation by weakening the father's responsibility for the care of his offspring thereby adding to women's burdens. These facts have implications of a most subtle kind for authority relations and for responsibility towards children and the home.

We have seen, then, that there are a number of demanding roles that a woman holds: those of worker, mother, wife and housekeeper. State-socialist societies have liberated women with respect to the first (of worker), but the roles of the other three are not in keeping with a position of equality to men. Women sacrifice occupational advancement to fulfil the other roles because the necessary reciprocation of men has not taken place. Women are not just unequal with relation to occupational advancement, but their burdens in the home and family are greater than those of men. I have mentioned the underlying cultural and traditional orientation of male superiority which is reproduced in these societies; it is important also to note that orthodox Marxism-Leninism as a critique of society is based on *class* struggle, and is insensitive to other forms of inequality, or to notions of a 'sex role', or relations between sexes. In orthodox Marxism-Leninism, work has a place of prime importance and it is undoubtedly true that access to a paid occupation has significantly enlarged women's social space; but having an occupation is only one of the ways by which individuals may be liberated. Hence this view of society does not provide an ideological springboard for a critique by so-called 'minority' groups (in a sociological sense) who may be unjustly treated and, as an ideology of socialism, rather than a critique of capitalism, orthodox Marxism-Leninism has many shortcomings. Perhaps of even greater importance is the fact that state-socialist societies are relatively poor countries: the economy needs women's work and the state for its reproduction requires the stability which a family may provide. What is perhaps questionable is the degree to which the burdens of work, housekeeping and child rearing in a socialist society should be borne disproportionately by the female population.

ETHNIC DIFFERENCES

An 'ethnic group' may be defined as a social group with a diverse range of traits including religious and linguistic characteristics, distinctive skin pigmentation and geographical origin of the members or those of their forebears (Tumin, 1964, pp. 243–4). The Soviet Union is a multilingual, multiracial and multi-national society being composed of many ethnic groups. In the 1979 census, of the 262 million people making up the population of the USSR, 137 million were Great Russian by nationality; and two other Slavic groups, the Ukrainians (42 million) and White Russians (9 million) were among the next three largest. There were eighteen other ethnic groups with more than a million people (see Table 3.10).

Study of population stock shows a disproportionate growth between European and Central Asian areas of the country. The natural increase in the USSR in 1977 was 8·5; in the Central Asia republics it ranged from 22·0 to 27·7 (for earlier periods see Feshbach and Rapawy, 1976, pp. 113–24). Another indicative statistic is that the gross reproduction rate in 1974 was 0·98 in the RSFSR and ranged from 2·33 to 3·07 for the Central Asian republics (1 equals reproduction of population). Not only do these data reflect geographical imbalances but a decline of the Russian, and a relative increase of non-Russian, ethnic stock.

It is extremely difficult to determine how far these groups enjoy differential status and prestige or are privileged or under-privileged in respect of political position. Soviet writers tend to emphasise the unity of the peoples living in the USSR and study the culture and way of life of ethnic groups rather than the more political interrelations.

Table 3.10   *National Composition of USSR Population (Millions)*

	Defined by nationality			
	1959 Census	*1970 Census*	*1979 Census*	%
Total population	208·82	241·71	262·08	100
Russians	114·11	129·01	137·39	52·38
Ukrainians	37·25	40·75	42·34	16·15
White Russians	7·91	9·05	9·46	3·61
Uzbeks	6·01	9·19	12·45	4·75
Tatars	4·96	5·93	6·31	2·41
Kazakhs	3·62	5·29	6·55	2·50
Azerbaydzhanis	2·93	4·38	5·47	2·08
Armenians	2·78	3·55	4·15	1·58
Georgians	2·69	3·24	3·57	1·36
Lithuanians	2·32	2·66	2·85	1·08
Jews	2·26	2·15	1·81	0·69
Moldavians	2·21	2·69	9·96	3·80
Germans	1·61	1·84	1·93	0·73
Chuvases	1·46	1·69	1·75	0·66
Latvians	1·39	1·43	1·43	0·54
Tadzhiks	1·39	2·13	2·89	1·10
Poles	1·38	1·16	1·15	0·43
Mordvinians	1·28	1·26	1·19	0·45
Turkmenians	1·00	1·52	2·03	0·77
Bashkirs	0·989	1·24	1·37	0·52
Estonians	0·988	1·00	1·02	0·38
Kirgiz	0·968	1·45	1·90	0·72
Other nationalities	7	9·10	3·11	1·17

Sources: Tsentral'noe (1962, pp. 184–9); *Naselenie* (1980, pp. 23–6). Percentages added.

'In our country, live and work in one happy family the representatives of more than a hundred nations and nationalities. In the USSR, for the first time in the history of mankind the nationality problem has been completely resolved' (*Strana Sovetov za 50 let: sbornik statisticheskikh materialov*, 1967, p. 19). Soviet political theory entails the abolition of national discrimination, but not of the nation as such. The Soviet writers Rogachev and Sverdlin have defined a nation as:

an historically evolved community of people, characterized by a stable community of economic life (if a working class exists), territory, language (especially a literary language),

83

and a self-consciousness of ethnic identity, as well as by some specific features of psychology, traditions of everyday life, culture and the struggle for liberation. (1966)

Soviet writers distinguish between two kinds of nations: the heterogeneous and the homogeneous. 'Bourgeois nations', it is suggested, are socially heterogeneous: they have bourgeois culture and a 'democratic culture of the working class'. Socialist nations, however, are of a different type; they are homogeneous:

> The economic basis of socialist nations is public ownership. A most important trait of such nations is their social homogeneity . . . Here an ethnic community is enhanced by a community of the fundamental socio-political interests of all members of the nation. The ideology of the working class becomes the ideology of the entire nation and the former duality of culture is surmounted. Unlike the socially heterogeneous nations, here arises a genuine and not an artificial community of the destiny of the entire nation. (Rogachev and Sverdlin, 1966, pp. 46–7)

Soviet socialist nations are considered to be of this kind. From this viewpoint, they are based on brotherhood, the distinctions between them are held to be cultural in character and thus membership of a 'socialist nation' does not bestow inequality, social superiority or inferiority, but simply distinctions of a cultural and linguistic kind; in short, nationality involves differentiation rather than stratification.

While accepting the cultural identity of the traditional nations making up the USSR, Soviet policy-makers have attempted to create a supra-national multiethnic concept of the Soviet nation, *Sovetski narod*. This involves a socialist community of different peoples united under a common state. It has the following features: a common territory (USSR), ideology (Marxism-Leninism), goal (communism), patriotism (Soviet) and proletarian internationalism. (See discussion in Rasiak, 1980, pp. 159–68.)

The concept of 'proletarian internationalism' points to another important implication of Soviet policy – that international conflict ceases to exist between socialist nations. The argument runs that 'bourgeois nations' pursue the policies of their ruling classes, whereas 'socialist nations' having no ruling class are able to follow peaceful policies. Many Western commentators deny the validity of this theory and argue that international conflict between socialist nations is not withering away. It may be caused by disagreements between such nations over economic exchange, over cultural dominance or over territory. The Chinese Communist Party in recent years has also adopted a similar criticism of the USSR's policies with regard to the border areas of China and to the Soviet involvement in Vietnam and their intervention in Afghanistan. These problems lie outside the scope of the present book. The extent of ethnic inequality in state-socialist societies, however, is of concern.

It would be surprising if there were equality of treatment of ethnic groups in the USSR. The Bolsheviks inherited a system of severe inequality between nationalities. Before the Revolution, in Central Asia, for example, only some 2 to 3 per cent of the native population was literate (Wheeler, 1964, p. 97), there were no institutions of higher learning and industrial development had hardly begun. The Soviet government attempted to reduce industrial and cultural inequalities and large-scale industry was set up in the underdeveloped areas. Between 1913 and 1935 in Turkmenia the industrial output of large-scale industry increased eight-fold, in Kazakhstan $8 \cdot 5$ times and in Kirgizia $8 \cdot 3$ times, whereas the figure for the USSR as a whole was $5 \cdot 7$ times (Schlesinger, 1956, p. 260).

Despite the inadequacies of the statistics and the low base, there has been a remarkable growth of industry in these previously backward areas though there are still considerable inequalities between the national groups. In 1961 while per capita income was equal to 100 in Latvia, it was $47 \cdot 7$ in Uzbekistan and $41 \cdot 8$ in Tadzhikistan (Nove and Newth, 1967, p. 42). Per capita consumption has undoubtedly increased in the non-Russian ethno-territorial regions; nevertheless, the increase in urbanisation has been greater in the 'Russian homeland' (RSFSR exclusive of mostly non-Russian autonomous republics) than in non-Russian areas: in the former between 1926 and 1970 it increased $41 \cdot 4$ per cent, in the latter by $27 \cdot 3$ per cent. By 1970 the Russian homeland was the most urbanised ethno-territorial area – in 1926 it ranked fifth (Clem, 1980, p. 209). Economic development during the time of Soviet power has not favoured consistently the underdeveloped non-Russian units. Much development has taken place in the Russian territories of the Urals, the Volga and Siberia and also in the non-Russian republics of the Ukraine and Kazakhstan. As Clem has pointed out, the ideological intention of industrialising and urbanising the 'underdeveloped' areas of the USSR has also had to take into account the maximisation of economic growth and development of heavy industry which favours the Russian homeland, and also strategic considerations militated against the development of the underdeveloped western areas of the country (Clem, 1980, pp. 209–11). While there may be unevenness in economic and social development between regions of the USSR, comparisons with developments in similar areas outside of the USSR invariably point to greater social and economic growth in the Soviet areas. Wilber (1969, p. 205) has shown that an effect of Soviet growth strategy has been for its Central Asian republics to outstrip countries like Colombia, India, Iran, Pakistan and Turkey which were at a similar level of economic development in 1926–8, to join France, Italy and Japan in 1960–2. Similarly, Libaridian has concluded that Soviet Armenia 'has been transformed by Soviet rule in a fashion unparalleled in the other countries of the Middle East' (1979, p. 38).

The upshot of these developments is that per capita income varies between republics, not so much because wage rates differ, but due to type of development and size of family. As will be seen from examination of Table 3.11, average monthly wages in 1978 did not vary greatly between republics – certainly not more so than in capitalist countries. On the collective farms, family income did differ considerably but the greatest variation was accounted for by family size: one may note how the very high family income (188 roubles per month) in Uzbekistan, fell to 69 roubles when individual members of the family were taken into account.

Educational provision has followed a similar trend. The non-Russian peoples have increased their chances of education, but have not yet reached the level of the Russians. An index of the

Table 3.11 *Indicators of Average Monthly Wages (1978) and Total Incomes on Collective Farms (1970) in Republics of USSR*

	1978		1970 Total Incomes on Collective Farms (Index)	
	Average Monthly Wages			
	Roubles	Index	Per Family	Per Family Member
USSR	160	100	100	100
RSFSR	168	105	102	109
Ukraine	146	91	80	92
Belorussia	141	88	84	94
Uzbekistan	148	92	188	69
Kazakhstan	160	100	148	110
Georgia	134	84	105	94
Azerbaydzhan	138	86	92	58
Lithuania	158	99	122	150
Moldavia	129	81	85	84
Latvia	161	101	115	162
Kirgizia	144	90	93	68
Tadzhikistan	141	88	95	55
Armenia	153	96	117	76
Turkmenia	171	107	153	90
Estonia	178	111	122	205

Source: Schroeder (1979, pp. 27, 36).

national composition of students in higher education in 1927, 1959, 1965 and 1974/5 is shown in Table 3.12. A figure over 1 denotes over-representation, and an index below 1 shows under-representation. The Tadzhiks, Kirgiz, Turkmen and Uzbeks have obviously bettered their 'national chances' for higher education. Some groups are still relatively more privileged – Russians, Georgians, Armenians and Jews. It ought to be noted that (even though their index fell) the total number of Jewish students rose from 51,600 in 1956 to 94,600 in 1965 but by 1974 there were 76,200. By 1970 the index of persons over 10 years of age having higher and secondary education (complete and incomplete) for various nationalities was as follows: Russians 508 (per 1,000), Ukrainians 476, White Russians 438, Uzbeks 412, Kazakhs 390, Georgians 578, Azerbaydzhanis 424, Lithuanians 353, Moldavians 338, Latvians 488, Kirgiz 400, Tadzhiks 390, Armenians 518, Turkmen 430 and Estonians 462 (Tsentral'noe,

1973, Vol. 4). The Soviet authorities have enhanced the chances of the non-Russian nationalities for higher education by instituting a nationality quota system of positive discrimination which tries to ensure a fairer balance between the national groups than would be the case if qualifications alone were considered.

Table 3.12   *Index of Student Composition by Nationality 1927, 1959, 1965, 1974/5*

Nationality	Index 1927	Index 1959	Index 1965	Index 1974/5
Russian	1·06	1·13	1·11	1·13
Ukrainian	0·69	0·75	0·81	0·83
Uzbek	0·11	0·82	0·83	0·70
Kazakh	0·07	0·94	1·06	0·96
Georgian	2·00	1·41	1·38	1·27
Azerbaydzhani	0·91	0·92	0·93	0·87
Kirgiz	0·12	1·00	0·80	0·84
Tadzhik	0·08	0·71	0·57	0·61
Armenian	1·81	1·07	1·14	1·05
Turkman	0·21	0·80	0·80	0·61
Jewish	7·50	3·73	2·18	2·31
Tatar	0·40	0·75	0·71	0·87
White Russians	–	–	–	0·82

Sources: 1927, 1959 and 1965 – Aspaturian (1968, p. 177). 1974 – calculations by author based on *Naselenie* (1980, p. 23) and *Narodnoe obrazovanie* (1977, p. 282).

The figures mentioned ignore the quality of educational institution attended. Because the more prestigious institutes and universities are located in the European parts of the Russian Republic, it is probable that they contain a lower than average proportion of the non-Russian nationalities. In addition to this, other kinds of traditional barriers to educational equality still linger so that, for example, while in 1970 the index (per 1,000 women) of Russian women with higher or secondary education was 487, for Kazakhs it was 332, Kirgiz 342, Tadzhiks 326 (Tsentral'noe, 1973, Vol. 4). Arutyunyan (1974, p. 52), on the basis of empirical research in Kishinev found differences between Moldavians and Russians. Of the latter nationality, 67 per cent considered that women should work rather than do household activities, whereas for Moldavians the figure fell to 57 per cent. Moldavians had a greater interest in their own folk (*narodnye*) music (79 per cent) and dances (81 per cent), whereas the proportions fell to 44 per cent and 40 per cent for Russian folk forms (ibid. p. 53).

Let us now turn to consider the relations between the most numerous Russian ethnic group and the others. Russians have been the most mobile group territorially in the USSR. They constitute significant minorities in the republics outside the RSFSR – on average they make up about 20 per cent of the population: notably 21·1 per cent in the Ukraine (1979 census), and 40·8 per cent in Kazakhstan. The Russians are located mainly in the cities and in the republican capitals (excepting Tbilisi and Erevan) where they make up over 20 per cent of the population. Over the USSR as a whole some 14 per cent of families are of mixed ethnic stock. This tends to encourage the maintenance and spread of the Russian language and a certain degree of assimilation to Russian nationality (see Kory, 1980, pp. 287–90). Between 1970 and 1979 the number of people in the USSR fluently speaking Russian as a second language rose from 17·3 per cent to 23·4 per cent (census data). It would be erroneous, however, to infer that the other languages of peoples in the USSR are in decline. Data collected in the censuses of 1979 and 1970 showed the following percentages of ethnic groups which considered their 'native language' to be the same as their national group: Ukrainians 82·8 per cent (85·7 per cent in 1970), Uzbeks 98·5 per cent (98·6 per cent), White Russians 74·2 per cent (80·6 per cent), Kazakhs 97·5 per cent (98 per cent), Tatars 85·9 per cent (89·2 per cent), Armenians 90·7 per cent (91·4 per cent), Georgians 98·3 per cent (98·4 per cent), Germans 57 per cent (66·8 per cent), Jews 14·2 per cent (17·7 per cent) (*Naselenie*, 1980, pp. 23–4). To maintain the 'purity' of some of the non-Russian languages, Russian words have been replaced by the vernacular. For instance: 'The Soviet Armenian language has been gradually cleared of common words transferred from the Russian. Academicians have been developing a vocabulary of scientific and technical terms derived from the wealth of the Armenian language' (Libaridian, 1979, p. 40).

Arutyunyan (1974, p. 56) makes the point that social position rather than simple ethnic origin strongly influences social attitudes. In an empirical study of residents in the Georgian Republic he found that in a research institute the number of mixed inter-ethnic marriages was 8–12 per cent, in a factory among workers it was only 2 per cent; of the first group of respondents a third to a half had friends of another nationality, whereas for the second group the comparable proportion was only one-fifth.

As to whether the greater interaction of ethnic groups associated with industrial development and population movement heightens tension between ethnic groups or whether it will lead, as many Soviet writers suggest, to the 'merging', to the internationalisation of culture and to greater tolerance is a question which we may only touch on here. R. A. Lewis has argued that the processes of modernisation 'appear to intensify ethnicity through such forces as transportation, communication and migration. As groups come into contact and competition with one another, ethnic differences are perceived. That heightens the feeling of ethnic identity of all groups involved and generally results in animosities and tensions' (1980, p. 306). This, however, is a contentious viewpoint. Rywkin has concluded to the contrary that Muslims 'encounter virtually no discrimination in living or housing. They enjoy equal or better opportunities within their own republics and elsewhere in the Soviet Union . . . [T]here are no second-class citizens, no man-to-man superiority. Modern Muslim national-religious feelings may conflict with Russian domination, but individual Muslims, including those responsive to such feelings, do not suffer from person-to-person discrimination' (Rywkin, 1979, p. 10).

Patterns of interaction between Slavic and non-Slavic groups have not been the subject of much study in the USSR. However, a work by Arutyunyan based on 2,500 interviews conducted in the Tatar Autonomous Republic sheds some useful light on the attitudes of Russians and Tatars to authority positions and to intermarriage. When asked: 'If you were given an opportunity to select a person in direct command over you, which [nationality] would you prefer?' Of those speaking only the Tatar language 12 per cent preferred a man of Tatar nationality whereas only 3·6 per cent of those speaking Russian preferred a person of their own nationality. When asked, 'Do you approve of marriages between Tatars and Russians? How would you regard such a marriage by one of your near kin (son, daughter, brother or sister)?' Of the Tatars, only 0·4 per cent considered such a match objectionable, compared to 3·6 per cent of the Russians. A further 14·9 per cent of the Tatars and 5·4 per cent of the Russians preferred marriage to take place between persons of similar nationalities but would not raise any objection to a mixed marriage. At the other end of the scale, 80·4 per cent of Russians and 69·4 per cent of Tatars believed that the nationality of spouses had no significance. Some interesting differences are brought out when the ethnic groups are subdivided into men and women, and into 'intelligentsia' and other workers. Of the Tatar male intelligentsia, 13·6 per cent had a negative attitude both to a direct boss being of a different national-ethnic group and to mixed marriages, whereas among the Russian male intelligentsia the proportions were 5·8 per cent and 14·7 per cent respectively. An even higher percentage of Tatar women who were also intelligentsia were opposed to these arrangements: 18·5 per cent had a negative attitude to being supervised by a Russian and 14·2 per cent were opposed to mixed marriages. Russian women of intellectual status also felt just as strongly about mixed marriage as did their Tatar counterparts, 14·2 per cent having a negative attitude, but only 9·8 per cent of them were opposed to having a direct supervisor of Tatar nationality. By contrast with the male intelligentsia, male workers were less prejudiced: of the Tatars, 9·3 per cent had a negative attitude to a person of a different nationality being in command over them, and 11·0 per cent felt similarly about mixed marriages; and among the Russian male workers the proportion fell to 2·8 per cent on both counts. Tatar women workers, on the other hand, had the highest 'negative scores' of all groups: 17·7 per cent had a negative attitude to having a Russian supervisor and 15·6 were against mixed marriages; of the Russian women workers the figures were much lower – 3·8 per cent and 7·6 per cent respectively (Arutyunyan, 1969, pp. 133–4).

The figures cited above sustain the view that there is mild social prejudice between national/racial groups in the USSR, and that it is greater among the Tatars than the Russians. One may confidently conclude that a fair number of Tatars do not like being told what to do by Russians, and that a minority regard intermarriage with some distaste. The research also indicates that social class cuts across ethnic origin and is a most significant variable in understanding inter-ethnic group relations.

POLITICAL ASPECTS OF NATIONALITY

Let us now turn to consider the political aspects of the nationality problem. To what extent, it might be asked, do the Slavic white nations dominate the others? It is often suggested that the counterpart of the dominant ethnic group in the USA, the WASPS (White Anglo-Saxon Protestants) are the SRAPPS (Slavic-stock Russian-born Apparatchiks; Brzezinski and Huntington, 1964, pp. 132–3). The grounds are that this ethnic group has superior access to positions of economic and political power and takes the most important decisions affecting the life of society. How valid is such a statement? First, we may consider the social background of the political élite. The ethnic composition of the Politburo-Praesidium and Secretariat of the CPSU between 1919 and 1935, between 1939 and 1963, in 1973 and in 1980 is shown in Table 3.13.

The predominance of Russians, the small and random representation of other nationalities and the decline of the Jews are the main facts brought out by the table: of the central apparatus of the Party in 1980 the Slavonic stock (Russians, Ukrainians, White Russians) constituted 82 per cent of the total membership. In 1972 the Slavic nationalities constituted 81·4 per cent of the CPSU Central Committee: their share of the population as a whole was 53 per cent. Of seventy-nine government officials in the Council of Ministers in May 1964, sixty were Russians, sixteen Ukrainians and three had other ethnic origins; and of forty-seven ministers in the Council in 1966, thirty-nine were Russians, six Ukrainians, one was a Tatar and there was one Armenian (*Deputaty verkhovnogo soveta SSSR*, 1966). In the Central Committee of the CPSU elected in 1981, 68 per cent of the voting members (N = 319) were Great Russians;

Table 3.13 *Ethnic Composition of Politburo–Praesidium and CPSU Secretariat*

Nationality	1919–35 as percentage	1939–63 as percentage	1973 as percentage	1980 as percentage
Russian	65	79	56	68
Ukrainian	0	10	16	7
Georgian	6	3	0	3·5
Armenian	3	2	6	0
Uzbek	0	2	4	3·5
Jewish	18	2	4	0
Finn	0	2	0	0
Latvian	0	0	4	3·5
Polish	3	0	0	0
White Russian	0	0	12	7
Kazakh	0	0	4	3·5
Azerbaydzhan	0	0	0	3·5

Sources: Columns 1 and 2 – Bialer (1966, p. 217); column 3 – Rakowska-Harmstone (1974, p. 5); column 4 – author's calculations.

the next most frequently represented nationalities were Ukrainians (14 per cent), and White Russians and Kazakhs (2 per cent each). Finally, I have analysed the biographies of the leading 100 officials of the USSR as of February 1981. (These included all members of the Politburo, Secretariat, chiefs of departments of the Central Committee, heads of Party institutions and publications, First Party Secretariat of the RSFSR, members of the Praesidium of the USSR Council of Ministers, heads of selected ministries and state committees and heads of selected area organisations, such as the trade unions – see Rahr and Scarlis, 1981). Sixty-nine were Russian, thirteen Ukrainian, three White Russian, three Latvian, two Bashkirs, and there were one each of Uzbek, Tatar, Kazakh, Azerbaydzhani, Armenian, Georgian, Jewish and Moldavian background.

At lower levels of the political system the representation of non-Russian nationalities is much higher. Of the total membership of the Communist Party of the Soviet Union in 1981, 60·0 per cent were Russian (52·4 per cent of total population), 16·0 per cent were Ukrainians (16·1 per cent), White Russians 3·7 per cent (3·6 per cent), Uzbeks 2·3 per cent

(4·7 per cent), Kazakhs 1·9 per cent (2·5 per cent), Georgians 1·7 per cent (1·36 per cent), Azerbaydzhanis 1·6 per cent (2 per cent), Lithuanians 0·7 per cent (1 per cent), Moldavians 0·5 per cent (3·8 per cent), Latvians 0·4 per cent (0·54 per cent), Kirgiz 0·4 per cent (0·72 per cent), Tadzhiks 0·4 per cent (1·1 per cent), Armenians 1·5 per cent (1·58 per cent), Turkmen 0·4 per cent (0·77 per cent) and Estonians 0·3 per cent (0·38 per cent) ('KPSS v tsifrakh', *Partiynaya zhizn'*, no. 14, 1981, p. 18). In the republics Rywkin has suggested that there is 'reverse discrimination', meaning that non-Russians enjoy preference over Russians in certain posts. These include the First Party Secretaries at all levels, members of the republican politburos are mostly of the titular nationality, 'most ministerial and government positions in general' (1980, p. 182) (including the important chairmen of republican Councils of Ministers), jobs in public relations and certain posts in local industry and trade. It is sometimes suggested that in Central Asia the indigenous population is 'often given preference [in the job market] over Europeans, unless the latter are the only ones having indispensable skills' (Rywkin, 1979, p. 9). Bialer (1980*b*, p. 214) in a study of 'native cadres' in the national republics for 1976 found that in the Party Central Committee bureaux and Praesidium of Council of Ministers of all national republics 252 or 75·8 per cent were of indigenous cadres; in Uzbekistan the figure was 76 per cent, in Latvia 74 per cent and in Georgia 94 per cent. Russians, however, occupy a number of key posts – they are invariably Second Party Secretaries, heads of the state security organs (KGB) and communications, and Russians are usually chiefs of factories under all-Union ministries. The commander of military forces in a republic is also usually Russian.

The existence and attempted incorporation of local indigenous élites has been noted by most Western commentators (Bilinsky, 1967; Bialer, 1966 and 1980*a*; Rakowska-Harmstone, 1974; Rywkin, 1980). While it is generally conceded that Russification is widespread, it is also the case that non-Russian nationalities, especially their intellectual élites, may have a heightened self-consciousness of their own nationalism. It would be mistaken, however, to assume that these groups are likely to advocate 'independence' or secession from the USSR. This is because the local indigenous élites have a sense of participating in the Soviet system and they would have a great deal to lose by its demise. They are likely to exert pressure for greater decentralisation and regional control (Rywkin, 1979, p. 13). There is still to be taken into account the legacy of some of Stalin's punitive policies. During the war seven nationalities were deported on the grounds of security and of collaboration with the Nazis to Siberia and Central Asia. This policy was officially denounced in the late 1950s (Conquest, 1967, pp. 102–8). Many of such deported groups, such as the Crimean Tatars, still claim the right to return to their former homeland, and have been the subject of appeals by Soviet 'dissident' writers, such as Sakharov. (See, for example, Radio Liberty Research 41/80; on the history of Crimean Tatars, see Fisher, 1979.)

On the basis of such a short review, one cannot come to very firm conclusions about ethnic stratification in the USSR. While the occupation of political élite positions is biased in favour of the dominant Russian nationality, at local levels this balance is redressed. There is evidence to suggest that some ethnic groups may be at a disadvantage in the economic and educational spheres. In social relations, it is again probably true that there is a mild form of social discrimination on national ethnic lines. In addition, it can hardly be denied that the Russian language is dominant. The lingua franca of the USSR is Russian, the capital of the state is in the Russian Federation and the tendency to centralisation (known also in federal states such as the USA) strengthens the power of Moscow. The language in the army is Russian and there is a greater component of Russian norms in *Soviet* culture than those of other ethnic groups (the pattern of ranks in the army, for example, derives from that of the Tzarist army). Hence in a cultural as well as in a political sense, the Russians are a dominant group. On the other hand, the nationalities come into their own in many localities, where their cultural life thrives and where the indigenous national groups, especially if in a majority, enjoy considerable political and social rights. They have greatly gained from Soviet power.

SUBJECTIVE EVALUATION OF STATUS

So far the statistics we have considered are only indirectly relevant to social interaction. When asked, people may say that certain occupations confer social esteem but we must also consider the way in which these attitudes are reflected in social relations and social action. To what extent do manual workers defer to professional men? In what ways, if any, are women treated in an inferior manner to men? It might be the case, for instance, that even though ranking of individuals by profession is similar in two societies, the actual social distance between the compared occupations is very different. Members of an officer corps or the civil service may be given an equally high 'ranking' but the consciousness of having the status of an officer or of a permanent civil servant might well vary. The specific authority of occupational roles may have very different consequences for other role positions. Obviously, the extent to which roles reinforce each other is an important element in social stratification. The fact that a person has an upper professional occupation or is high on a certain ranking scale (income) does not necessarily mean that he will be deferred to or be given respect by all those who have lower positions or incomes. Here, then, we are concerned with the impact of the division of labour on other social relations.

This is a crucial aspect of social stratification into which very little systematic research has been carried out. It requires not the description of objective inequalities but consideration of how people rank others and themselves, and examination of how, in practice, incumbents of given roles relate to one another, of an analysis of how superiority and inferiority are reflected in social activity. The value system of a society defines in broad terms the desirable modes of action: Christians should play the good Samaritan to the downtrodden, Soviet Communists should have relations of 'mutual respect between individuals – man is to man a friend, comrade and brother' (*Programme of the Communist Party of the Soviet Union*, 1961, p. 79). In the Soviet value system, it is axiomatic that particular occupations or levels of income should not elevate some men over others. In theory, individuals are merely differentiated from one another and not stratified in terms of social worth. In other words, the status and role of an individual in relation to the means of production and exchange should not, in a socialist form of society, give rise to a consciousness of membership of a social stratum (or class) which shares common values, attitudes and interests, and which considers itself as superior or inferior to other strata. Ideological statements, however, are no sure indication of the way individuals or groups do act. Soviet sociologists have been concerned with the development of a socialist personality, with a 'new socialist man' (*Dukhovoe razvitie lichnosti*, 1967). Their writings have concentrated on the educational and cultural levels of different social groups, rather than on the interaction between individuals and groups and their differential perception of the social structure. Though it would be interesting to describe the statuses of individuals in different positions, no Soviet work has been carried out into these relationships. It is possible, however, to gain some insight into these aspects of life from contemporary literature and expatriates; and from such accounts there would appear to be considerable conflict between those in authority and those subject to authority.

One may also make some inferences about the nature of social relations by studying patterns of friendship and marriage. It might be expected that in an egalitarian society friendship and marriage would be formed independently of occupation, educational background or level of income. On the other hand, if friendship networks and intermarriage occurred predominantly between those of similar social background, this might indicate the existence of social barriers and social distance between groups.

Connor (1979, pp. 270–3) has usefully assembled data about intermarriage in Czechoslovakia, Hungary, Poland and the USSR. These are shown on Table 3.14. Husbands and wives are arranged in four groups according to their present occupations and divided into 'élite' (1), 'routine non-manual' (2), worker (3) and peasant (4). The Czech figures relate to a survey conducted in 1964 (N = 110,150), the Hungarian to 1963 (N = 5,939), the Polish to a mid-1960s study –variant I refers to a survey of 1,594 and includes non-working wives, variant II (N = 1,060) excludes such wives. The Soviet research is from a 1966 study of Estonia (N = 1,515).

Overall these figures show a fairly high degree of homogamous unions when considered in broad groupings. The median figure for élite husbands marrying women from the same group was 38·2 per cent (of course, the number of 'élite women' is small); if one combines the wives in groups 1 and 2, then a range of from 66·8 per cent (Czechoslovakia) to 97·5 per cent (Poland II) were in the non-manual category. Studying the occupational backgrounds of manual workers' wives, from 50·3 per cent (Hungary) to 85 per cent (Poland) were in the same group. In the USSR (87 per cent) and in Hungary (97 per cent) of peasant men chose wives of the same social category.

A Soviet study of educational attainment of spouses showed a high positive correlation (+0·66). It was found that 93.4 per cent of the men with higher education had married women with middle and higher education and, at the other end of the scale, 65·2 per cent of men with less than elementary education had married women at the same educational level (Aganbegyan, Osipov and Shubkin, 1966, pp. 200–1). In a study of 1,000 Leningrad divorces, 77·3 per cent of the couples belonged to the same social group which, if it is at all representative of all marriages, confirms the above (Kharchev, 1965, p. 163). Again a Polish study of the educational backgrounds of 1,401 married couples found that spouses had very similar educational backgrounds. Of women with higher education, 87 per cent had husbands of the same educational standing, and 93 per cent of the wives of men with incomplete primary education had received a complete primary (25 per cent) or incomplete primary (68 per cent) education (Lobodzinska, 1970, p. 8).

A Hungarian study of graduate engineers shows that they mainly make friends with people of a similar educational and professional background: as many as 86 per cent of young chemical engineers' best friends were graduates mostly engaged in similar professions. The same study confirms that marriage takes place between spouses of similar occupational backgrounds. The wives of the chemical engineers were also largely selected from similar occupational groups (Szesztay, 1967, pp. 154–5). In the Soviet Union, Shkaratan (1970, p. 428) found

Table 3.14 *Socio-Occupational Categories of Wives, by Category of Husbands, Various Socialist Countries*

Husband	Wife			
	1	2	3	4
1 Élite				
Czechoslovakia	38·2	28·6	30·5	2·7
Hungary	16·0	56·9	16·0	11·0
Poland I	48·2	48·2	3·6	–
USSR	38·2	30·9	26·6	4·3
Poland II	63·3	34·2	2·5	–
2 Routine non-manual				
Czechoslovakia	21·7	37·6	37·6	3·1
Hungary	3·6	52·9	32·9	10·6
Poland I	11·1	71·2	17·7	–
USSR	7·7	53·3	27·7	11·3
Poland II	7·9	79·6	12·5	–
3 Worker				
Czechoslovakia	9·7	14·6	67·8	7·9
Hungary	0·8	10·5	50·3	38·5
Poland I	1·0	23·0	76·0	–
USSR	4·9	17·5	65·8	11·8
Poland II	0·6	14·4	85·0	–
4 Peasant				
Czechoslovakia	5·6	6·2	38·8	49·4
Hungary	0·0	0·0	3·0	97·0
USSR	1·4	4·3	7·3	87·0

Source: Table constructed by Connor (1979, p. 271). Adapted from Vladimir Srb, 'K dynamice socio-profesionalni heterogamie v CSSR', *Sociologicky casopis*, vol. 3 (1967), table 6; Central Statistical Office, *Social Stratification in Hungary* (Budapest: CSO, 1967, p. 126); Wielislawa Warzywoda-Kruszynska, 'Zbieznosc cech spolecznych wspolmalzonkow', in K. M. Slomczynski and W. Wesolowski (eds), *Struktura i ruchliwosc spoleczna* (Wroclaw, Warsaw, Krakow, Gdansk: Wydawnictwo Polskiej Akademii Nauk, 1973, pp. 132–3; M. Kh. Titma, 'The influence of social origins on the occupational values of graduating secondary-school students', in Murray Yanowitch and Wesley A. Fisher (eds), *Social Stratification and Mobility in the USSR* (White Plains, NY: International Arts and Sciences Press, 1973 pp. 182–3).

that members of various strata choose close friends from the same or similar social groups. In the three highest strata, some 60–70 per cent of the respondents had friends from the same groups; of the unskilled manual workers, more than 78 per cent had their best friends in the manual-worker stratum.

We may conclude that in state societies no less than in Western ones there is significant differentiation of interest and outlook between people from various backgrounds which strongly influences their choices of friends and spouses. The high rates of marriage within certain occupational groups, together with the evidence from the research (see pp. 69–70) on the aspirations of children, would also suggest that the offspring of different strata are socialised into quite different subcultures. This has been put quite explicitly by the Soviet sociologists Gordon and Klopov who conclude: 'in the workers' milieu strata are being distinguished ever more distinctly which differ . . . by their level of culture in the broad sociological sense of this term as a designation of the totality of life conditions, norms, traditions, and knowledge directly determining man's behaviour' (1973, p. 33).

A more intractable area of study of social stratification lies in the ways that individuals perceive class position. Research into the perception of class position was conducted in Poland in 1958 and was based on a sample of workers in six industrial enterprises and five other groups (the Ministry of Education, a hospital clinic, and craftsmen, sailors and young people at a youth camp). Of those objectively 'working class', 92·6 per cent considered themselves to be of that class. The ideology bestowing prestige on workers probably accounts for this very high figure. Of the 'intelligentsia' who had come from this background, 79 per cent considered themselves to be 'intelligentsia'; on the other hand, of the intelligentsia who originated in the manual strata only 37·6 per cent considered themselves to be members of the intelligentsia, the majority assigning themselves to the 'working class' (Widerszpil *et al.*, 1959). What makes the Polish results even more remarkable is the fact that the surveys were carried out only fourteen years after the creation of a state-socialist society. Of course, in the Polish countryside the peasantry would probably not have identified themselves as 'working class' to the same extent as non-manual workers.

Gordon White (1978, p. 561) has described the attempt by the leaders of the Chinese People's Republic to change the status hierarchy as a 'dynamic political process'. Policy and activity of the leaders during 1949 to 1956 attempted to turn on its head the pre-revolutionary status hierarchy. Social honour was redistributed to the advantage of the labouring classes and in its place a new hierarchy was to be constructed with industrial workers at the top and the former upper classes were to occupy a lowly social position. The impact of such policies was limited for a number of structural reasons. The 'legacy of history' could not be changed overnight and differences in prestige construed to be associated in the traditional way to those from town and country and to those in manual and mental labour. Changes did take place, honour and status in the new occupational division of labour increasingly became associated with income, skill, authority and type of work (ibid., p. 566). Wesolowski and Slomczynski in a study of male workers in Poland found that a majority of respondents 'claimed to ascribe equal prestige to all occupations, but believed that others did not'. The self-proclaimed egalitarians, however, 'actually assigned prestige differentially' (cited by Lipset and Dobson, 1973, pp. 141–2). In fact status is linked to occupation and the level of education.

Wage inequality is 'built in' to the structure of state socialism and it is interesting to study the attitudes of different groups towards it. A Polish survey (Glowacki, 1959) may be summarised as follows. The great majority of manual workers thought that the government should set limits to wage differentials and believed that the existing differentiation in Poland was both too great and was unjustified. Examples of the kinds of argument favoured by these relatively lowly paid egalitarians are that 'everyone has the same stomach and same right to live', and that 'a director and a cleaner have the same needs'. Some of them also advanced explicitly political arguments of the following kind: 'as all are to be equal under communism so wages should not differ'; 'a too high differentiation in wages divides into classes which as time passes are becoming hostile to each other'; 'the worker under communism should not be so badly treated'. The majority of technical and administrative personnel was also in favour of limiting wage differentials, but here a sizeable minority (one-fifth) was against such a policy. The views of the majority also exhibited more varied and sophisticated reasons: such as that 'the difficulties arising for the state should be equally spread over all citizens', and that 'everyone tries to fulfil his duties well, so wages should not differ much'. But the majority of the technical administrative group wanted greater differentials between lowest and highest incomes than did the manual workers; and those who opposed an upper limit argued that the existing limits were insufficient incentive for maximum effort. The third group of respondents, those with higher education, tended to favour both higher differentials (from 5:1 to 10:1) and even the removal of a ceiling. The arguments they used are familiar in Western societies: 'it is necessary to have incentives for greater effort and [to enhance] educational improvement'; 'it is worth giving a few thousand more to a good director or engineer [for] the profits may be in millions'; 'in building and industry the difference is too little and even in an opposite direction from what it should be'.

Another study carried out in 1973 of 394 employees of a large enterprise in Krakow came to similar conclusions: some 57 per cent of production managers thought that differentials should stay as they were; of the unskilled workers only 20 per cent thought so, and 54 per cent wanted a reduction in differentials compared to 31 per cent of the managers (data cited by Kolankiewicz, 1979, p. 20). Only 10 per cent of the respondents thought that 'within 30 to 40 years all incomes should be levelled regardless of work or position' (none of whom were managers).

As Glowacki points out, personal conditions had an indubitable relationship to egalitarianism: the lower the income and education, the greater the claims for egalitarianism; and the higher the education and income, the greater the wish for hierarchy.

Estimations of social worth also varied by social class. Manual workers believed that miners and foundry workers deserved the highest salaries – higher even than those of scientists, other experts and political leaders. The technical and administrative personnel (without higher education) put in first place highly qualified experts, then scientists, factory managers, political leaders. The engineers and other personnel with higher education would have given the highest salaries to scientists, the creative intelligentsia and those in leading government posts – in that order; and very few of this group ranked miners and foundry workers at all highly.

This research from Poland thus highlights the conflicts that exist over the distribution of the economic surplus between the various social strata. After the initial political process by which the capitalist owners of industry were expropriated, conflicts arise between the new élites (including the highly qualified professional groups and the Party *apparat*) and the majority of the manual workers. The latter invoke 'communist ideology' to support egalitarian wage claims which would give them benefits, while the intelligentsia seek to further their cause by reference to their superior contribution to the national welfare. Even those in intermediate positions rationalise their own self-interest by reference to general social goals. These empirical facts point up a contradiction between the 'official ideology', according to which the 'working class' is politically and socially unitary, and the fact that income is distributed differentially between various groups making up that class. At the same time, it is interesting to note that these groups are able to articulate more or less opposing views which rationalise their different interests, despite the unifying objective of the official ideology.

On the basis of the evidence presented above we may make a number of observations which modify the 'official' view of social stratification. Although income inequality in countries of the Soviet type has a narrower span than in capitalist societies, there is, nevertheless, a considerable variation in the actual consumption patterns of different social strata which indicates a marked differentiation of lifestyles. Status differentiation appears to be related very closely to occupation and education and while the range of 'social distance' may be narrower in state-socialist countries than in Western capitalist states (though this has not been very satisfactorily proven) a generally similar rank ordering of occupations occurs. Inequalities between the sexes and between nationalities also persist. Furthermore, what facts we have about patterns of marriage and perceptions of differential rewards strongly suggest that state-socialist societies do have a definite system of prestige and that individuals regard themselves as members of distinctive status groups.

4 Social Mobility and Political Class

The foregoing chapter has been concerned with the hierarchical arrangement of social groups and with the nature of inequalities between them. We shall now turn to consider the extent to which such differences may have crystallised to form more enduring social groups. In the present chapter we shall use what empirical material there is available to consider whether a ruling class or political élite is ensconced at the apex of the power structure. It might be objected, of course, that it is not possible to 'test' such general theories in one chapter of a short book for they require a profound analysis over time of many aspects of the society we are describing and, in addition, much critical information is not available in systematic and reliable form. However, despite these objections, we might consider two indicators of group crystallisation. First, we may study the extent to which upper professional and executive occupations are open to recruitment from manual and unskilled non-manual strata. Secondly, we may examine the social composition of the political élites which will give us some indication of the extent to which there exist self-perpetuating ruling groups.

THE RECRUITMENT OF THE INTELLIGENTSIA

A characteristic of a democratic occupational structure is that leading and intellectual occupations are both desired and actually open to all children independently of their social background. One might expect, other things being equal, that the distribution of children in professional occupations would not vary with the occupation of their fathers. Social mobility should provide avenues for upward and downward movement such that one social group would not monopolise the desirable positions. But social mobility is not only linked to democratic values, it is considered by many sociologists to be an important component furthering the stability of modern society. It is sometimes argued that upward mobility reduces social dissatisfaction and frustration and therefore furthers social stability (see, for instance, Bendix and Lipset, 1959). Conversely, restriction of mobility may not lead to individual dissatisfaction, but may also weaken the capacity of the élites to rule because capable, and possibly aggrieved, people may pose a political threat to them.

Sociologists usually distinguish between structural mobility and exchange mobility. Structural mobility is caused by the number of actual statuses increasing – say through industrial and economic development – and calling for an inflow (see above, Chapter 1). Exchange mobility entails that the number of positions remains the same and the social origins of the occupants of those positions change. Industrialisation following the seizure of power by the Communist Party tends to be most intensive with very high rates of growth. In Russia, for example, between 1922 and 1940, non-manual strata as a whole increased at an annual rate of 16·7 per cent per annum. As the economy matures, the rate of growth tends to fall and this reduces the rate of occupational mobility – in the USSR, between 1960 and 1972, the annual average increase of non-manual positions fell to 5·8 per cent. Hence the rate of structural mobility declines.

A Polish survey (sample of 3,482 non-agricultural households: Zagorski, 1970) has attempted to compare social mobility in prewar and postwar Poland. A summary of some of the results is shown in Table 4.1. The table shows that, comparing the situation before the war with that between 1956 and 1968, a large increase took place in both the proportions of industrial manual and non-manual workers hailing from a farming background: for the former the proportion rose from 22 per cent before 1940 to 39·9 per cent between 1956 and 1968; the share of children from agricultural backgrounds taking non-manual work rose from 18·3 per cent to 30·5 per cent. The share of non-manual workers with fathers in industrial-manual work only rose slightly from 24·2 per cent before the war to 26·1 per cent between 1956 and 1966. Movement from non-manual into manual jobs, however, was very small, rising only from 4 per cent to 5·7 per cent between the prewar and postwar periods, showing that the

Table 4.1   *First Jobs as Manual or Non-Manual Workers outside Agriculture according to Fathers' Socio-Occupational Group at that Time (Poland)*

	Respondent's socio-occupational group when taking first job			
	Industrial-manual workers		Non-manual workers	
Father's socio-occupational group	Year work was commenced			
	Before 1940	1956–69	Before 1940	1956–69
	%	%	%	%
Farmers or agricultural labourers	22·0	39·9	18·3	30·5
Manual workers outside agriculture	66·3	48·1	24·2	26·1
Non-manual workers	4·0	5·7	43·3	36·4
Private handicraftsmen, etc.	4·3	2·1	9·2	2·6
No data	3·4	4·2	5·0	4·4
	100·0	100·0	100·0	100·0
N	323	700	120	341

Source: Adapted from Zagorski (1970, p. 4).

children of non-manual parents tend to stay in non-manual jobs. Upward social mobility, therefore, has been stimulated by the increase in non-manual and manual jobs outside agriculture resulting in a general upward movement of men from industrial manual and agricultural backgrounds, rather than a large downward movement of non-manual strata.

A comprehensive picture of intergenerational mobility accompanying rapid industrialisation is given by a study of the Yugoslav census carried out in 1960 (Milic, 1965). Milic shows that considerable upward mobility took place. Of the non-manual workers, the largest single group (40·4 per cent) had fathers who were peasants; this was also the case with the manual workers – 57·3 per cent originated in the peasant stratum. The doubling of the industrial population between 1953 and 1961 was largely due to an inflow of peasants from the countryside. At the same time, however, there was considerable self-regeneration of each stratum. This is particularly apparent for the peasantry: 92·6 per cent of the peasant respondents had peasant fathers; of the children of manual industrial fathers, the largest group (58·3 per cent) also became industrial workers – though they formed but a third (36·8 per cent) of the total of that group. The children of non-manual workers also largely (67·3 per cent) became non-manuals, though again they formed less than a third (30 per cent) of the total number of non-manual workers.

If we examine in more detail the internal characteristics of the very widely defined 'manual industrial' and 'non-manual' strata we see that the inflow of men from lower strata fills the least skilled positions. For instance, Milic shows that of the total of unskilled manual workers, 74·5 per cent were of peasant origin, the proportion falling to 48 per cent of the skilled and highly skilled manual workers (ibid., p. 124). In white-collar jobs, 84·2 per cent of the low-grade office employees and auxiliaries were of peasant or manual industrial origin; but of those with the highest qualification, 51·1 per cent were the offspring of non-manual parents.

Similar trends have been found in Poland. Zagorski (1974) in 1972 studied a 0·5 per cent sample of Poland's economically active population. The study showed a predominantly 'upward' profile of mobility. There was a large outflow of farmers' sons to manual (31·3 per cent) and a lesser number (12·1 per cent) to non-manual occupations. While 61·5 per cent of the children of manual workers also become manual workers, 27·5 per cent entered non-manual jobs, and formed the largest group (38·8 per cent) among such workers; and of non-manuals' sons, 68·3 per cent became non-manual workers. The sons of non-manual workers, however, also experienced downward mobility – some 27·3 per cent became manual workers, though they accounted for only 5·8 per cent of the total number of manual workers.

Taking recruitment to specific professions, Zagorski also shows that there is a definite tendency towards internal recruitment. Physicians and stomatologists make up 0·4 per cent of the economically active population, though a quarter of this occupational group also had fathers who were physicians and stomatologists; scientific workers and teachers account for 0·2 per cent and 1·9 per cent of the economically active population, and the proportion of workers in these fields who also had fathers in them is 17·4 per cent and 19·6 per cent respectively (Zagorski, 1974, p. 17).

Considering mobility to different kinds of non-manual jobs between 1950 and 1972, Zagorski shows that there is a tendency for internal self-recruitment to decline over time. For instance, the percentage of children of administrative and managerial fathers starting their first jobs in the same occupational group was 33·9 per cent in 1950–4, 22·8 per cent in 1965–9, and 21·7 per cent in 1970–2; children of 'specialists in technical fields' entering the same socio-occupational group were 22·7 per cent of the cohort in 1950–4, 17·9 per cent in 1965·9 and 19 per cent in 1970; the children of 'specialists in non-technical fields' entering similar posts fell from 39·3 per cent in 1950–4 to 35·2 per cent in 1965–9 (it was 35·3 per cent in 1970–2) (Zagorski, 1974, p. 15). Of course, these data relate to first jobs, and to make this point more convincingly one would need also to know the ultimate destinations of these children.

EDUCATIONAL OPPORTUNITY

Soviet data are not as comprehensive as the Polish and we have to rely on local studies which have been mainly concerned with educational opportunity for different social groups. These studies, however, generally point to similar trends to those in Poland. A survey of 9,000 youths carried out in 1976 in Lithuania came to similar conclusions regarding aspirations. Some of the results are shown in Table 4.2. The table shows the overall high level of aspirations of all school-leavers for education. Examination of the table brings out the much 'higher' levels of the children of middle-class 'specialists' – from 73 to 94 per cent of this group sought a place in an institution of higher education, not one gave first place to going directly to work. It was among the collective farmers' offspring that desire for a technical college was greatest. Similarly, a study by Shubkin (1965, 1966) shows not only that it is the 'intelligentsia' who have the highest aspirations for their offspring but that the actual achievement of their children outstrips that of other social groups. In Shubkin's study 76 per cent of agricultural workers'

Table 4.2 Aspirations of School-Leavers in Lithuania, 1976

Social Origin	Place of Abode	Higher Education	Technical Institute (Tekhnikum)	Trade School	Work and Study	Work	Residual
Workers	Village	41·1	41·1	11·0	3·5	2·2	1·1
	Small Town	62·4	30·4	2·0	5·0	–	0·2
	Large Town	43·4	14·2	3·2	9·7	0·5	29·0
Collective Farmers	Village	34·3	44·5	10·6	5·7	2·3	2·6
	Small Town	47·9	44·8	2·1	4·2	–	1·0
	Large Town	46·0	23·0	7·7	15·4	7·7	0·2
'Middle-Class' - Specialists	Village	72·7	18·2	6·1	–	–	3·0
	Small Town	73·3	20·0	–	2·2	–	4·5
	Large Town	94·2	1·5	–	3·1	–	1·2

Source: Gentvaynite, Matulenis and Talyunayte (1977, pp. 74–6).

children and 93 per cent of the offspring of the urban intelligentsia wanted to continue to study: these desires were subsequently fulfilled by only 10 per cent of the first category and by 82 per cent of the second. Research into the social background of university students in 1973–5 revealed that 36·7 per cent were the children of workers, 7·2 per cent were of collective-farm and 54·6 per cent of white-collar background. Of school-leavers whose fathers had higher education 76·9 per cent entered university, compared to 26·2 per cent with fathers of primary education (Filippov, 1977, p. 49).

A more detailed study showing the social background of students by educational institutions reveals some interesting facts (see Table 4.3). Study of this table not only confirms what was said above on unequal class chances, but it also shows the prevalence of certain social groups in particular faculties. Students from white-collar homes are particularly well represented at the university, the law institute, teachers' institute and conservatory. Those from working-class background are more frequent at the polytechnic, the mining, the railway and the economics institute. Though these figures refer to correspondence- and evening-course students, among all students a similar tendency operates.

A study in 1976–8 of some 15,000 students in the RSFSR and Baltic republics by Filippov (1980, p. 90) confirmed these trends. He found that only 3·3 per cent of university graduates in humanities' faculties originated from the families of collective and state farmers, the figure rose to 18 per cent in natural sciences, 18 per cent in teacher training, 44·3 per cent in agriculture and 5·5 per cent in medicine. (Comparative data for Czechoslovakia and Poland are given in the same source, pp. 90–1.) A study of the social composition of the student population in Kharkov showed that in 1974/5, 47 per cent had a working-class background, 39 per cent were white collar (*sluzhashchi*) and 13 per cent were children of collective farmers (Sheremet, 1977, p. 77). The author also points to differentiation in the various faculties: in the creative arts, the children of workers constituted 32 per cent, collective farmers 3·4 per cent, and those from a white-collar background were 64·4 per cent; in medicine the comparable figures were – 44·5, 21·0, 34·5; in

Table 4.3 Social Background of Students in Higher Education by Institution and form of Study, Sverdlovsk, 1966

Institution	Evening Students				Correspondence Students			
	N	Manual workers or children of manual workers	Peasants or children of peasants	Non-manual workers or children of non-manual	N	Manual workers or children of manual workers	Peasants or children of peasants	Non-manual workers or children of non-manual
		%	%	%		%	%	%
Polytechnic	5,913	63·8		36·2	9,073	45·2		54·8
Mining institute	929	54·9	2·6	42·5	4,018	58·4	0·4	41·2
University	2,069	21·7	0·6	77·7	2,692	34·8	10·2	55·0
Railway institute	1,534	64·1		35·9	4,277	38·3		61·7
Law institute	1,027	37·4		62·9	4,868	17·2	0·3	82·5
Economics institute	170	57·1	5·3	37·6	1,810	51·1	0·1	48·8
Teachers' institute	277	31·8		68·2	3,015	3·5		96·5
Conservatory	82	24·4	3·7	71·9	248	35·9		64·1
TOTALS	12,001	52·5	0·4	47·1	30,001	36·6	0·9	63·5

Source: Protsessy izmeneniya sotsial'noy struktury v Sovetskom obshchestve (1967, pp. 133, 139).

agricultural institutes, 49·6, 34·3, 16·1; in building, 58·8, 8·0, 33·2, and in transport, 62·1, 6·9, 31·0. In industrial institutes in 1974/5, 60 per cent of the students hailed from working-class background (no other data given). Therefore it might be inferred that relatively more upward mobility takes place for manual workers in industrial than in non-industrial occupations. This is illustrated by a study of occupational mobility in a Moscow electrical engineering plant which showed that of 1,000 workers who began as semi-skilled operators, after ten years, 295 were engineers or technicians and 680 skilled operators. Of 34 men who had entered the factory ten years previously as apprentices, 14 had been promoted to the position of engineer or technician (Guryanov, 1966, p. 127).

Within the upper professional occupations, there is considerable horizontal mobility and mainly in the direction of scientific and technological employment in the sons' generation. Seventy-three per cent of sons where fathers had graduated in the humanities aspired to posts in physics, mathematics and technology, 22 per cent to other natural sciences and only 5 per cent to jobs in social science, history, literature and language. Of sons having fathers with professional qualifications in physics, mathematics and technology, 88 per cent aspired to their fathers' professions, 12 per cent to other natural sciences and none wanted a career in the humanities. Girls of higher professional origin, on the other hand, were more attracted to the humanities. Of the daughters of mathematicians, physicists and technologists, 39 per cent wanted the same profession, 29 per cent other scientific jobs, and 30 per cent preferred the humanities; whereas among daughters with fathers in the humanities, 50 per cent wanted a similar profession, while 21 per cent preferred physics, mathematics and technology, and 26 per cent other scientific professions (Aganbegyan, Osipov and Shubkin, 1966, p. 221). Another study showed that in the higher creative arts the children of non-manual workers do well. Of members of artistic professional associations in Belorussia 77 per cent of composers, 68·9 per cent of architects, 59 per cent of cinema professionals, 47 per cent of painters and 25 per cent of writers had non-manual origins (*Struktura Sovetskoy intelligentsii*, 1970, p. 104).

It is now appropriate to consider the ways that the school and the family influence children's success in the educational system. Because Soviet schools are unstreamed and comprehensive, the structure of the school would appear to be egalitarian. In theory, the school seeks to raise all children up to a common average standard. Children from poorer home backgrounds, therefore, might be thought to benefit most from this system while those from a superior intellectual home environment may not be fully extended. But despite the comprehensive-school system there is considerable difference in the attainment of children and Aganbegyan, Osipov and Shubkin (1966) have shown that success at school is correlated with parents' education and social position. For boys, the correlation coefficient relating success at school and mothers' occupation is $+0 \cdot 31$, and for girls the correlation between mothers' education and school success is $+0 \cdot 32$ (p. 204). In his study of the Tatar Republic, Arutyunyan found a correlation of $0 \cdot 7$ between the educational level of parents and children (cited by Lipset and Dobson, 1973, p. 167). A study in Novosibirsk which related children's school grades to their social background showed that the offspring of parents with higher educational qualifications did much better than those of other social groups: on average 5 per cent of all children got 'excellent' marks but this figure rose to $11 \cdot 4$ per cent in the case of the children of parents with higher education, and the comparative figures for 'good' marks were $30 \cdot 5$ per cent and 43 per cent for the two groups respectively (Musatov, 1967, p. 47).

As in Western societies, home background also influences the age at which children leave school. In Nizhny Tagil it was found that children of workers made up 72 per cent of the school intake, 60 per cent of the eighth form, 55 per cent of the ninth form and $44 \cdot 2$ per cent of the eleventh form (*Klassy, sotsial'nye sloi i gruppy v SSSR*, 1968, pp. 206–7). Filippov's (1977, p. 49) comprehensive study of students in higher education in the USSR showed a similar tendency for the drop-out rate of students at universities to be higher for the lower social groups: of students in the first-year courses, $31 \cdot 2$ per cent were from worker's families, $8 \cdot 4$ per cent from peasants, $44 \cdot 8$ per cent from white-collar backgrounds; the comparable figures for students graduating were $26 \cdot 2$ per cent, $9 \cdot 7$ per cent and $61 \cdot 5$ per cent. Considering the students in his sample who attended universities, those of white-collar background constituted $51 \cdot 7$ per cent of the first-year course and $70 \cdot 2$ per cent of those leaving (ibid., p. 50). A Hungarian survey (Ferge, 1966) strikingly brings out the unequal stratum chances of staying in education: while 83 per cent of children of the upper professional group remained at school after the compulsory minimum age, this figure fell to 37 per cent for the children of skilled workers, to 15 per cent for those of unskilled workers, and to 18 per cent for those of agricultural labourers.

The importance of father's education as a determinant of occupational career of sons has been illustrated quantitatively by Safar (1971) as a result of his research in Czechoslovakia. The coefficient between father's occupation and son's (first job) was only $0 \cdot 12$ (comparative figure for England and Wales ($0 \cdot 12$)) whereas it rose to $0 \cdot 49$ ($0 \cdot 24$) when the link between father's education and son's education was measured. The index between father's occupation and son's present job was only $0 \cdot 02$ ($0 \cdot 17$) which rose to $0 \cdot 50$ ($0 \cdot 33$) when son's education and son's present job was studied. (Data cited in Heath, 1981, p. 218.) Heath suggests that these data show the importance of cultural capital in socialist states which modifies the apparently open achievement pattern of such societies.

Consideration of the studies so far would seem to point to three conclusions: with the maturation of the industrialisation process there is a tendency (1) for the replenishment of occupational strata from within those strata (that is, children 'inheriting' their parents' social position), (2) for upward mobility to continue, but at a slower rate, and (3) for downward mobility from non-manual to manual to increase. There is no evidence to support a thesis that the able children of manual workers are denied access to higher education and therefore may present some actual or potential political opposition.

These studies are an indication of the amount of gross mobility; we have not discussed measures of 'exchange' as against structural mobility. Connor (1979, p. 175) has done a useful calculation of mobility rates in many state-socialist and capitalist countries by separating out mobility caused by structural change from that of exchange. Table 4.4 shows some of the main results. Here we may note that the measure of exchange movement upwards is much less in socialist than in capitalist countries and also that rates of downward exchange mobility are higher. Of course, these results are unrealistic in the sense that structural change and the mobility associated with it do characterise present socialist states.

Table 4.4   *Basic Mobility Indicators, National Data Adjusted to Eliminate Structural Changes*

	Manual to Non-manual	Worker to Non-manual	Farm to Non-manual	Non-manual to Manual
Bulgaria	4·6	11·1	2·0	64·0
Czechoslovakia	6·5	14·1	4·1	65·6
Hungary	4·3	8·3	1·8	61·0
Poland	5·3	10·7	1·9	64·4
Rumania	4·2	12·7	1·4	30·6
Yugoslavia	5·3	14·2	2·8	57·6
France	17·6	29·0	6·4	37·3
Italy	10·8	20·1	4·3	34·8
Great Britain	24·8	–	–	42·1
USA	15·7	22·0	5·8	49·5

Source: Connor (1979, p. 175).

We might conclude this section by saying that while upward social mobility has undoubtedly been very great in state-socialist societies in recent years, it has been largely a result of industrialisation and the creation of many new positions, both manual and non-manual. Factors have also been in operation which seem to limit downward intergenerational mobility. Children from urban areas and from the higher professional and other non-manual families have not only better access to cultural facilities but also higher aspirations. Family background makes more 'educable' the children of parents with higher educational and professional attainment. The educational system to some extent operates to negate the political ideals of equality. The political élites may stress equality of educational opportunity, but the educational system itself tends to seek to produce as efficiently as possible properly skilled and motivated manpower; and to do this it selects students who will benefit most from the use of its scarce resources. Hence the modern educational system, whose main function it is to train and to allocate labour, has direct selective effects on the system of social stratification. While a lower proportion of children from manual backgrounds compared to non-manual aspire to higher education, there is nevertheless a considerable absolute number who do so, and some may find their desires frustrated by the superior educational performance of the non-manual employees' children – they are the losers in a competitive achievement selection system. While these tendencies may be counteracted to some extent by unstreamed comprehensive education, such measures cannot fully overcome the inequalities of opportunity created by differences in family milieux. We may generalise that with the greater economic maturity and political stability of the kind of societies under consideration there is a tendency for the higher social strata to be self-recruiting, though there is some evidence to suggest that downward mobility may increase. In the absence of any significant increase in the rate of industrial development or major political changes in state-socialist societies, one might expect the pattern of social stratification to become more stable and the amount of upward mobility to decline.

At the same time, one cannot realistically assume that the many strata forming 'the intelligentsia' are a unitary social group. Though it may be conceded that some strata are accorded certain privileges – for they have high income, they are often in control of other men and their jobs often give them high status – they are not a homogeneous category. In particular, the cultural and technical intelligentsia is said to be subject to political control: writers, for instance, are subject to censorship, social scientists' research is often not published and scientists' projects (and even their visits abroad) may be determined by the government. Therefore, it is important to discuss separately the social background of the political élites, the top men in the Communist Party and ministerial apparatus, to see from which levels of society they originate and whether they are a self-perpetuating group.

POLITICAL RECRUITMENT

The Communist Party of the Soviet Union (and analogous

parties in Eastern Europe) which may be said to perform the function of aggregating political interests, is widely believed to be the dominant political institution in Soviet society. There are two aspects of this crucial organisation to be considered in the present context: first, the social composition of the Party, and secondly, the 'placement' role of the Party in respect of positions in other institutions. One should bear in mind, however, that one cannot simply infer a class interest from data on the social composition of the élites. Whose interests are served by the political leadership may only be discovered by an interpretation of the effects of policies executed, which is outside the scope of this book.

Table 4.5   *Social Structure of USSR (Official Figures) and Social Composition of CPSU*

	Social structure of USSR		Party composition		
	1959	1979	1956	1968	1981
	%	%	%	%	%
Manual and non-manual workers	68·3	85·1	82·9	84·2	87·2
Of which: manual	49·5	60·0	32·0	38·8	43·4
non-manual	18·8	25·1	50·9	45·4	43·8
Collective-farm peasants	31·4	14·9	17·1	15·8	12·8
	99·7*	100·0	100·0	100·0	100·0

* An additional 0·3 per cent of the population was self-employed in agriculture and handicraft work.

Sources: Semenov (1964, p. 258). Party composition 1968: *KPSS* (1969, p. 9), Tsentral'noe (1980, p. 8); for 1981: *Soviet Weekly*, 7 March 1981. In 1981 the Party had a total membership of 17·48 million – 9·3 per cent of the adult population. 1979 census data: *Vestnik statistiki*, no. 1, 1981, p. 66.

Study of Table 4.5 shows that non-manual workers (25 per cent of the total population in 1979) constitute the largest group in membership of the Party (43·8 per cent in 1981). The share of manual workers in the Party has increased in recent years. At the 26th Party Congress (1981), Brezhnev announced that in the five years preceding the congress, 1·5 million manual workers (59 per cent of those joining) were from the blue-collar strata. This situation is paralleled in Poland where in 1966 non-manual workers accounted for 42·6 per cent of the membership of the

Polish United Workers Party (PUWP), the share of manual workers was 40·2 per cent, and peasants 11·7. By 1979 manual workers made up 46 per cent of the membership (1·3 million) and the non-manuals had fallen to 33 per cent (Sadowski, 1968, pp. 93–4; Kolankiewicz, 1980, p. 4). The higher grades of non-manual workers, particularly scientists and researchers, are likely to be Party members and many statistics have been collected to show the extent of Party 'saturation' of these kinds of posts. A study of the Party background of Soviet local government deputies found the following steep gradation of Party membership according to occupation: factory directors 99 per cent, 'sub-directional management' 51 per cent, foremen and other junior supervisory posts 38 per cent, specialists lacking administrative powers 27 per cent, workers 18 per cent. These figures, of course, relate to the more politically inclined personnel who also take part in local government (Rigby, 1968, pp. 433–9). This trend continued up to the 1980s when it was reported that 20 per cent of the USSR's 'specialists' were Party members, two-thirds of those with higher degrees, and half of the candidates of science (i.e. university graduates); approximately 10 per cent of all manual workers were Party members (*Soviet News*, 24 February 1981); 42 per cent of qualified engineers, 25 per cent of teachers, and about the same proportion of physicians are also in the Party. Thus the CPSU is not socially representative of the population of the USSR: the non-manual strata, particularly the executive and professional occupations, are over-represented and the collective-farm peasantry are underweighted. The manual working class has a substantial membership (about 10 per cent of all manual workers), but relatively fewer Party members than its share of the total population.

The figures on Party membership overall, however, refute the view that the Party is an unrepresentative 'élitist' group – 27 per cent of all Soviet citizens with ten years' schooling and over 30 years of age are Party members, and this figures rises to 44 per cent of males with these characteristics (see also, Bialer, 1980*b*, pp. 188–92).

At the level of the political leadership people with white-collar occupations, as in all industrial societies, play a more dominant role. At the Party Congress in 1981 there were 5,002 delegates:

1,370 (27 per cent) were workers from industry, 877 were 'workers in agriculture', 609 were *khozyaystvennye rukovoditeli* (managerial staff) including 358 managers, 1,077 (21·5 per cent) were Party officials (*Pravda*, 26 February 1981). In 1966 the Central Committee of the Party had 195 full members and 165 candidate members. By 1981 the membership of the Central Committee had risen to 470 (319 full members and 151 candidates). Of the voting or 'full' members, 90 per cent have higher education – and this figure includes fifteen members of the USSR Academy of Sciences and twenty-five with higher degrees – and, unlike in Western politics, the majority of these people (60 per cent) had degrees in science and a minority (22 per cent) higher qualifications in arts.

This mainly male company included the most powerful people in the USSR – full-time Party Secretaries, chiefs of government departments, army officers, police chiefs, trade union and Young Communist League leaders, heads of leading industrial enterprises, members of the Academies of Science, representatives from the arts, as well as the editors of some of the major newspapers. A broad breakdown of the institutional background of Central Committee members in 1981 (1976 in brackets) was as follows: N = 470 (426); Party apparatus 41·3 per cent (41·3); government apparatus 31·1 per cent (32·6); military 7·2 per cent (6·8); diplomatic service 3·8 per cent (3·8); state security 1·3 per cent (1·4); academic and cultural specialists 4·3 per cent (4·7); trade unions 1·7 per cent (1·6); 'labour aristocracy' 7·7 per cent (5·6) (Teague, 1981). The political élite, therefore, is largely composed of top officials from Party and government bureaucracies. The size of the Central Committee has been regularly enlarged (total members 235 in 1952, 470 in 1981) to 'incorporate' representatives from the major institutional and professional interests in Soviet society.

The political élite is composed of a score or so men (none is, or has been, a woman) ensconced in the political bureau (or Politburo). Their institutional affiliation has changed over time and since the demise of Stalin the Party in the shape of full-time Party officials has secured control. In 1951 in Stalin's Politburo ten out of eleven men were from the government apparatus (though four held joint Party posts); only one (Khrushchev) was exclusively from the Party apparatus. By 1981, of the fourteen full members, nine have Party posts and five are from the government apparatus.

The social background of the élites is difficult to analyse because Soviet biographies often exclude 'social origin'. Hough has examined a sample of biographies (185) of leading officials of the Central Committee. He concludes that the younger cohorts of top officials are more likely to be of middle-class background than the older ones: of those born 1900–9, 45 per cent were from workers' families, 41 per cent from peasant background and 14 per cent were white collar. Of those born 1910–18, 26 per cent were of proletarian origin, 39 per cent hailed from the peasantry and 35 per cent were white collar (1979, p. 7). What is clear is that the officials now coming into the political leadership have a more homogeneous educational background than the older men. Of those born 1917–20, 63 per cent had completed full-time education, compared to 93 per cent of those born 1930–7 (the youngest cohort) (ibid., p. 12).

The educational profile of the Politburo has also been transformed in the past thirty years. Of the 1951 Politburo, six men had received an elementary education, one had a secondary technical and two had incomplete higher technical. By 1981 all its members had higher education and ten out of fourteen had received a higher technical education. Study of the educational background of these men shows that nearly all came from provincial technical institutions: unlike the British Cabinet which is drawn largely from men from the élite universities of Oxford and Cambridge, in the 1981 Politburo only one and the youngest (Gorbachev) had graduated from Moscow University. It might be noted here that the tendency of the Politburo to recruit men of university education was also true in four East European countries. Between 1949 and 1967 the percentage of members with higher education rose from 33 to 55 in Poland, from 0 to 39 in Hungary, 19 to 36 in Czechoslovakia; in Bulgaria, however, it fell from 33 to 25 (Farrell, 1970, p. 96).

Study of the social origins of the political élite does not show that they yet form a hereditary class or ruling group – at least as far as social recruitment patterns are concerned. Bialer (1980*b*, p. 179) has examined the social origin of leading Soviet officials in the Party and state apparatuses between 1956 and 1966. Of those holding positions in the Politburo, Party Secretariat, Praesidium of the Council of Ministers and the Praesidium of the Supreme Soviet, 87 per cent were of worker or peasant origin, of the Central Committee the proportion was 73 per cent, of the Council of Ministers 76 per cent, of provincial and republican Party–state leaders 82 per cent; of 'key economic managers' and 'key military commanders' the figures were 72 and 74 per cent respectively. In Schneller's study (1966, p. 105) of the twenty-seven members of this Politburo between 1917 and 1951, eight were the sons of manual workers, seven originated from the peasantry, seven had a non-manual background and five were of unknown social origin. Comparing these data with the social origins of the members of the Politburo between 1966 and 1981 we may conclude that there has been very little change. In 1971 the social origins of twenty-one full and candidate members were: manual working class nine, peasantry seven, non-manual workers four, unknown one. By 1981, of the full members five were working class, six peasants, three non-manuals.

Of great importance is the extent to which the Party allocates men to other positions in various parts of Soviet society, for in this way it may have considerable power to shape the pattern of social mobility. We have seen in earlier chapters that one of the most important changes which limited the ascription of position was the nationalisation of property, which meant the elimination of inheritance of substantial wealth, and of private ownership of the means of production. But such ownership relations are not unique determinants of status, power and privilege. We have seen that after the October Revolution, administrative mechanisms allocated privilege to previously deprived classes. Then, as now, the Communist Party selected and allocated personnel to all positions of power in Russia by making appointments and elections to higher positions in state-socialist societies subject to 'Party control'. In practice, the cadres (or personnel) department of the Party's Secretariat exercises the placement function. It may actively suggest individuals for certain positions and it may also veto the appointments made by the 'cadres' departments of other institutions. In view of this practice, some writers have argued that Party administrative selection in state-socialist societies replaces the kind of ascription on the basis of ownership which occurs at the highest levels of capitalist societies.

Few comprehensive data are available to us on the actual operation of the Secretariat in its placement function. Party control is exercised in two ways: by influencing the selection of people put forward for elective positions in the Communist Party, the Soviets (Parliaments) and trade unions; and by sanctioning appointments to executive posts in organisations (offices, factories, the army, etc.) which come under the various government ministries. No Soviet empirical research is available on the extent of this process of social selection. For some posts, officials are appointed by the Party, whereas for others the approval of, or ratification by, a Party body is all that is necessary. Party oversight pertains not only to some 3 million posts having administrative and executive importance, but also to elective posts in the Soviets, unions and collective farms, and to delegates to conferences (Harasymiw, 1969, p. 511). However, just what constitutes 'control' is very obscure. It is often asserted that the Party penetrates other structures so that

> party career divisions within both the state bureaucracy and the party bureaucracy are much more significant than the division between these bureaucracies. In fact, there is such a high degree of interchange between the middle levels of the state and party bureaucracies that it is impossible to look upon these organizations as separate élite segments. Moreover, the principal line officials of both state and party are so closely associated by both training and career as to constitute a single body. (Armstrong, 1959, p. 144)

Studies of the career paths of Party Secretaries and factory directors would suggest, however, that the lines between Party and governmental careers are now more firmly drawn. Stewart's study (1968) of a sample of 208 Party Secretaries who held their positions between 1950 and 1966 shows that prior to becoming officials they had worked in a variety of occupations. The following figures show the limited extent to which they were transferred, as might be generalist administrators, to important positions in the state apparatus. Of the careers studied of 202 local First Secretaries, Stewart shows that only 4 were 'promoted' to positions in the federal government apparatus, that is, as chairman or deputy-chairman of the USSR Council of Ministers and USSR minister or deputy minister, and 31 were 'transferred' to similar positions in the republican government apparatus. On the other hand, 64 were promoted to higher positions in the Party apparatus. Another study by Hough of the chairmen appointed in 1957 to the Regional Economic Councils (*sovnarkhozy*) shows that out of a sample of ninety-seven men (about whom biographical data were collected) only six had previously been Party officials, and the remainder had been recruited from senior administrators and executives in government service. Also, in considering the background of the directors of important plants, Hough found that all but one had had an engineering background – and forty-six out of forty-eight biographies showed that they were graduate engineers. Moreover, these men had risen within the industrial hierarchies; in 1958 they were men in their late 40s or early 50s 'with three decades of experience in industrial management' (1969, pp. 58–9, 62).

Thus work of Stewart and Hough modifies considerably Armstrong's view, stated above, that Party and state bureaucracies might be considered as a single body. But perhaps even more crucial than interchange at the middle and regional levels of administration is the social background and career paths of the ministers who guide the economy of the USSR and to whom we shall now turn.

Table 4.6   *Career Paths of Ministers in USSR Council of Ministers (1966 and 1981)*

	1966	1981
Having career in government organisations	37	47
Having career in Party, Komsomol, trade union and government organisations	10	24
Unknown	0	7
	47	78

Sources: Based on biographies in *Deputaty verkhovnogo soveta SSSR* (1966), *Deputaty verkhovnogo soveta SSSR* (1979) and other biographical sources.

In Table 4.6 I have collected data on the leading ministers of the USSR (chairmen and deputy chairmen and all having ministerial posts) for 1966 and 1981. Distinguishing simply between those who had worked in government institutions and those who had worked in Party/*Komsomol*, trade union *and* government institutions, we see from their career paths that nearly four-fifths had had a career exclusively in government institutions. Even of the ten who had held posts outside (in Party, *Komsomol* – Young Communist League – or union) three had been *Komsomol* officials only during an early part of their career and had subsequently made a full-time career in government service. Also, between 1950 and 1965, only five had switched between higher Party and government jobs. By 1981 two out of three ministers would have had a lifetime's experience in a government department. There has been a tendency since the 1960s for more 'switching' of positions to take place, and Brezhnev has strengthened the hand of the Party by bringing in men from this institution. Since 1965 seventeen of the seventy-eight ministers in office in 1981 (April) have had a dual career. But the days of élite domination by Party generalists are over. As Bialer (1980*b*, pp. 120–1) has concluded (following his own empirical study): 'The overwhelming majority of individuals in the post-Stalin generation show a very low degree of mobility with regard to both type of job and geographical location.'

We might fairly confidently conclude that the heads of the Soviet ministerial system are career specialists. The evidence indicates that most Soviet ministers have a relevant higher education and have spent most of their working lives in their own ministry. While it is too sweeping a statement to say that a rigid structural differentiation takes place between Party and government administration, the evidence cited above leads us to conclude that there is a tendency to internal recruitment within the Party and ministerial hierarchies.

It is outside the scope of this short book to consider in detail the extent of political conflict between the various élites in state-socialist society. (The points which follow have been dealt with at greater length in Lane, 1978, chs 7 and 8.) But the evidence presented above suggests that the Communist Party does not ascribe positions in governmental institutions as a reward for political activity, though it still has a certain amount of patronage at its disposal: appointment to managerial and scientific positions is determined by education and qualifications; it is meritocratic rather than ascribed by the Party authorities. Nevertheless, one of the main cleavages in state-socialist society is between those groups whose authority lies in the Communist Party (for example, Party Secretaries) and others whose position is technocratic and professional. Parkin, in discussing Poland, Hungary, Czechoslovakia and Yugoslavia, has noted the 'quite sharp antagonisms . . . between the younger generation of graduates and technocrats on the one hand and the older party veterans and partisans on the other . . . In Czechoslovakia . . . opposition to the economic reforms came from factory managers whose appointment owed more to their politics and proletarian origins than to their technical abilities' (1969, pp. 365–7). We saw earlier in this chapter that with the maturity of the state-socialist system, the social structure becomes less flexible and more rigidly stratified with benefits and advantages accruing to the professional, executive and technical groups. Party activists believing in classlessness and equality may articulate policies through the Party *apparat* which seek to redress the balance of the power between them and such groups (Feldmesser, 1966, pp. 527–33). Such a cleavage between Party *apparatchiks* and ideologists, on the one side, and professionals and technical specialists, on the other, is a dynamic factor in the internal politics of state-socialist society. The development of a 'market' form of economy will obviously enhance the power of the technocrats and professionals and at the same time reduce the influence of purely Party functionaries. (See also discussion on Poland in Hirszowicz, 1980, ch. 5). Consideration of the composition of the political leadership points to the ambiguity of the notion that the socialist state acts 'on behalf of' the working class. This is because the 'working class' under socialism is anything but a homogeneous group, except perhaps in the sense that all its members are 'employed' for wages. The actual direction of the economy and the rewards it distributes must be seen in relation to the *stratification* of the working class and particularly the representation of various interests in the Party and government apparatuses.

125

5 Class, Cleavage and Control

In the preceding chapters we have seen that sociologists in socialist states consider social stratification from the point of view of hierarchy rather than dichotomy, of harmony rather than conflict, and regard differences in income, power and prestige to be justifiable in terms of the efficient and effective operation of present-day socialist society. Their arguments, often couched in Marxist terminology, legitimate inequalities in the social order. Other writers interpret social relations in a more critical way. They emphasise conflict between the ruling classes (or élites) and the masses and regard the various forms of inequality as essentially illegitimate and exploitative and in no way 'necessary' for the efficient and effective management of society. There are three main approaches which will be discussed in turn: neo-Marxist models, a neo-Weberian approach and a totalitarian-mass model.

NEO-MARXIST CONFLICT MODELS

Under this heading we may distinguish three different variations. First, the view of Trotsky and his contemporary exponent, Ernest Mandel: they characterise Soviet-type societies as 'degenerate workers' states'. Secondly, the paradigm of 'state capitalism' articulated by Rizzi and more recently by Tony Cliff. Thirdly, there is the notion that state-socialist societies represent a new type of social formation, which is put forward by Hillel Ticktin, or a novel mode of production arising out of the Asiatic mode of production – a view associated with Umberto Melotti.

Trotsky accepted Marx's definition of classes as being 'characterised by their position in the social system of economy and primarily by their relation to the means of production' (1945, p. 248). He agreed that the class character of the Soviet Union was 'proletarian' – in so far as this had been guaranteed by 'the nationalisation of the land, the means of industrial production, transport and exchange, together with the monopoly of foreign trade . . .' But Trotsky denied that the interests of the proletariat were being served by the incumbents of political power. In particular, he distinguished between the interests of the proletariat and its political organisation, the Communist Party, and the interests of those who were in the commanding positions of the bureaucracy. It was the bureaucracy, he argued, which had lodged itself in an exploitative relationship over the working class.

Arguing from Marxist theory, he held that under capitalism the bureaucrats who run the government and the capitalist corporations play a subservient role to the ruling property-owning classes. But in Soviet society the working class which was 'hardly emerging from destitution and darkness, [had] no tradition of domination or command' and therefore such a bureaucratic group was able to manipulate its position to become 'the sole privileged and commanding stratum in Soviet society' (1945, pp. 248–9). But although the polarisation of socialist society was between this group and the working class, the dominant exploiting stratum was not a class in the Marxist sense for it had 'neither stocks nor bonds. It is recruited, supplemented and renewed in the manner of an administrative hierarchy, independently of any special property relations of its own [and] the individual bureaucrat cannot transmit to his heirs his rights in the exploitation of the state apparatus' (p. 249). Though the relationship between the political leadership and the masses is not harmonious, the kinds of inequalities discussed earlier in this book do not amount to antagonistic class relations but are rather bourgeois-like types of unequal distribution caused by the inadequate level of productive forces (Mandel, 1969, p. 14; idem, 1980, pp. 120–1).

In Trotsky's view this privileged stratum did not have the characteristics of ruling classes in the classical Marxist sense. The Soviet order was not (and still is not) capitalist. As the leading exponent of contemporary Trotskyism has put it:

State ownership of all important industrial, transportation

and financial enterprises (i.e. of the means of production and circulation) combined with legal (constitutional) suppression of the right to their private appropriation, centralised economic planning and state monopoly of foreign trade, imply the absence of generalized commodity production and of the *rule* of the law of value in the USSR. This means that the economy is no longer capitalist. There is neither a market for large means of production nor for manpower, and labour power has ceased to be a commodity. (Mandel, 1980, p. 118)

According to Trotsky, the privileged layer seeks 'to conceal its income' and in denying its own existence it is 'equivocal and undignified'. The dominant ideology of Marxism-Leninism does not justify bureaucratic rule and acts as a restraint on the power of the ruling stratum. Trotsky's theory does not assume that the masses are aware of the polarisation of power and wealth. Here, then, we have a situation in which individuals may not be conscious of the way exploitation takes place. They are manipulated. They may think that they take the decisions even though effective power is denied them, or they may believe that society is based on equality whereas in fact they are exploited. However, Trotsky held that with its maturation the working class would come to perceive the objective opposition of interests in the society and would overthrow the bureaucracy by revolution.

Trotsky and his followers do not accept the diachronic scheme put by Soviet Marxists, described above. Rather than a progression from the revolution through the dictatorship of the proletariat to socialism, they describe uneven change. The economic achievements of the USSR by 1936 are acknowledged:

Gigantic achievements in industry, enormously promising beginnings in agriculture, an extraordinary growth of the old industrial cities and building of new ones, a rapid increase of the number of workers, a rise in cultural level and cultural demands – such are the indubitable results of the October Revolution, in which the prophets of the old world tried to see the grave of human civilisation . . .

Socialism has demonstrated its right to victory, not on the pages of *Das Kapital*, but in an industrial arena comprising a sixth part of the earth's surface – not in the language of dialectics, but in the language of steel, cement and electricity. (Trotsky, 1945, p. 8)

Politically, however, they saw the Soviet Union as degenerating. Trotsky's supporters point out that from the time of the suppression of the Kronstadt revolt (1921) (though supported by Trotsky) democracy began to be undermined, it suffered a terrific blow when Trotsky's opposition to Stalin was defeated (1923) and when Trotsky himself was deported in 1929. The purges of the 1930s were in Trotsky's view the culmination of despotism and Stalin's claim to have achieved socialism by 1936 was blatantly false. Socialism could not be reached in one country alone, especially in a backward society such as the USSR. For capitalism, it was argued, was supra-national in character and its contradictions would penetrate the Soviet Union to make impossible the development of society on a qualitatively higher (socialist) level. To achieve socialism Trotsky considered that a revolution was necessary in other advanced capitalist countries. Such a revolution would create the economic and political basis for socialism on a world scale.

Depending heavily on Trotsky's analysis, but extending it in some important respects, is the bureaucratic class model expounded by Rizzi (1939), Djilas (1966), Schachtman (1962), Ticktin (1973), Kuron and Modzelewski (1968), Carlo (1974), Melotti (1977 and 1980) and Meikle (1981).

Rizzi (1939) is usually credited with the first 'state-capitalist' explanation of the USSR. He was followed by Burnham (1941), Tony Cliff (1964), and Binns and Haynes (1980). (For further discussion, see Bellis, 1979.) Unlike the traditional Trotskyite theory which depicted a ruling *stratum*, this theory emphasises the domination of a new bureaucratic *class* over the working class. It is argued that, whereas under private enterprise capitalism individual shareholders own the means of production, in societies organised on the Soviet model, it is the state which has the formal powers of ownership. But the state as a collective body is controlled by bureaucrats who have *de facto* control of the state.

> History has seen examples of class and antagonistic societies in which state ownership of the means of production has prevailed (the so-called Asiatic method of production).
>
> State ownership of the means of production is only a *form* of ownership. It is exercised by those social groups to which the state belongs. In a nationalised economic system, only those who participate in, or can influence, decisions of an economic nature (such as the means of production, the distribution of, and profiting from, the product) can affect the decisions of the state. Political power is concerned with power over the process of production and the distribution of the product. (Kuron and Modzelewski, 1968, p. 6)

This class, 'the central political bureaucracy' (p. 15), acts as a ruling class and like the bourgeoisie under capitalism, the economic surplus which it extracts from the workers gives it social and economic privileges. Moreover, it is able to justify its leading role by an adaptation of Marxism to an ideology of class consensus which serves to stupefy the working class.

Like Trotsky's view of Soviet development in the 1930s, Kuron and Modzelewski see the early phases of state-socialist industrialisation in Poland as corresponding 'to the demands of economic development and the general interests of society' (p. 26). The achievements of the industrialisation process, however, entailed the transformation of the political order into a 'class dictatorship by the bureaucracy'.

> It may be said . . . that the nature of the task of industrialising a backward country called to life as a ruling class a bureaucracy which was able to achieve this task, since it alone, through its class interest, represented the interest of industrialisation under such conditions – production for the sake of production. (p. 27)

In contrast to the Soviet theory considered in Chapter 1, the bureaucratic model sees class rule being strengthened by industrialisation and urbanisation which provide the basis for the extraction of surplus by the bureaucratic class from the workers.

Cliff and other state-capitalist theorists concede that Soviet-type societies do not have competition between firms (between capitals); rather the state bureaucracy becomes one collective capital. The drive for accumulation (and hence exploitation of the working class) is derived from the external world capitalist economy and functions through military competition and arms production: 'competition through buying and selling is replaced by direct military competition' (Cliff, cited by Bellis, 1979, p. 145; on the permanent arms economy see Bellis, 1979, pp. 144–50).

The later developments of this approach have led to the conclusion that 'Soviet-type' societies are not capitalist, nor socialist, nor transitional, but are a new form of bureaucratic class domination representing either a new type of social formation or mode of production. Rather than being a variant of capitalism ('state capitalism') they are an alternative mode of development. Melotti defines 'bureaucratic collectivism' as a 'modern class society based on specific relations of production that set workers and bureaucrats at opposite sides. Characterised by an enlarged production (similar to capitalism's), bureaucratic collectivism is clearly different from all pre-capitalist societies of simple reproduction (ancient, Asiatic, or feudal) as well as from traditional capitalist society, which sets the proletariat against the bourgeoisie. As with all class societies, bureaucratic collectivism can be distinguished by its specific forms of exploitation' (Melotti, 1980, p. 174). Rather than seeing a progression: primitive communism → ancient → feudal → bourgeois → communist (see above, p. 6), Melotti claims that in Russia and China the progression has been primitive commune → semi-Asiatic → bureaucratic collectivism, which may subsequently lead to socialist society, thence to communist society. Bureaucratic collectivism, then, is an alternative and parallel mode of production to capitalism (see Melotti, 1977, chs 1 and 2). Ticktin and Meikle do not see the Soviet Union as a new mode of production but as a 'form of hybrid' – 'the product of a transitional epoch between modes of production, the product of conflict between the laws of the declining mode and those of the social relations of the invading mode, but which is a historical blind alley thrown up by the conflict without itself having any tendency of motion towards the new mode of production' (Meikle, 1981, p. 107). Unlike Trotsky, Ticktin and Meikle do not regard Soviet-type societies as being dynamic and progressive; rather they view them as stagnant, 'moribund' and 'an obstacle to the process of world revolution' (ibid., p. 108).

It seems to me that these theories, though deficient in some respects, illuminate many inadequacies in the 'official' Soviet theory. To begin with, the general point that control of the means of production rests in relatively few hands is well taken. The failure to acknowledge the possibility of political control being vested in a bureaucracy is a serious shortcoming of the Soviet theory and one that has had serious consequences for the Soviet political élite itself. For if there are no 'antagonistic contradictions' then it may be argued that there cannot be any need for a ruling political party to maintain the hegemony of one class (the working class). This was the basis of the justification of the forms of 'pluralism' which were introduced in Czechoslovakia by Dubcek in 1968, when the 'guiding' role of the Party was to be replaced by a more open and pluralistic political system.

However, since the Soviet intervention of Czechoslovakia, a theoretical justification of continuing Party hegemony has been made. Glezerman (1968) has argued that classes are groups of people who can appropriate the labour of others due to the position they occupy in the company. According to this theory, it might be possible for a particular stratum, say the cultural intelligentsia, to mislead the population by virtue of its control of communications. This tendency might originate in the bourgeois origins of such strata. Therefore, says Glezerman, the political arm of the working class, the Party, must continue to safeguard the interests of the people and prevent a resurgence of capitalism and bourgeois nationalism. The Czech 'progressive' Communists, on the other hand, argued that there was a fundamental unity of interests between the intelligentsia and the working class, and that rather than the intelligentsia destroying the fabric of a socialist society it was the hegemony of the Communist Party expressed in the bureaucracy that was an anachronism. Regardless of the truth of these two points of view, Glezerman has conceded that the control of a state-socialist society is a separate issue from ownership and that, as bureaucratic theorists have pointed out, groups in élite positions may not have the same interests as the workers. But bureaucratic critics, of course, would go much further and argue that the Party élite itself is an exploiting class or stratum.

A second criticism of Soviet theory that is raised by the critics discussed above relates to the formal Marxist view of class. The point has already been made that in Marxist theory the relations of production are only one element which constitutes the basis of society, the level of technology being the other. Since the 'material forces' of Soviet (and other East European) society are not more highly developed than in the advanced capitalist countries, it is therefore open to question whether social relations can be at a higher level than those of capitalist countries, as the Marxist notion of a socialist system would have it.

Another disputable aspect of the Soviet theory is concerned with the notion of ownership. Ownership is a legal term defining the exclusive right of the individual to command over, dispose or enjoy the possessed object. Now the Soviet distinction between state and private property is a misleading one. For state ownership in fact does not convey equal rights to all citizens to enjoy and dispose of property. Government ministries and various organisations are given rights to the utilisation of state property and these, in turn, give certain groups of individuals prerogatives which others do not have. Such rights over property are stringently enforced. Thus while one might concede that the Soviet state does indeed have the right to distribute resources, the control of property is differentially distributed in state-socialist society and the consciousness of property remains. However, it is important to recognise that private ownership is limited to personal possessions and does not have the significance that it does under capitalism where it includes ownership of capital. For the analysis of the structure of the system of state socialism as a whole one should not conflate private ownership of possessions with private ownership of capital and confuse both with state control of property. As a characteristic determinant of class position, individuals in state-socialist societies lack property (capital) in a Marxist sense.

The work of Melotti points to the peculiar historical trajectory of Russia and China and the impact of its previous 'Asiatic' forms on their present organisation. Whether this leads to a new 'mode of production' is questionable, but the point may well be taken that the cultural, organisational and political processes have origins in national and traditional formations and are not necessarily 'socialist'.

The 'conflict theorists' described above are also open to serious criticism themselves. In the first place, Trotsky's theory is unclear about the constitution of 'bureaucracy'. It could be a horizontal grouping of incumbents of positions at the apex of the Party, the ministries and the Soviets (parliamentary organs). On the other hand, it could be a vertically integrated set of positions, such as the ministerial apparatus. If the bureaucracy is a horizontally integrated group, it would have to be shown that Party Secretaries and ministerial *nachal'niki* (heads) had an actual, rather than a possible or potential unity of interest, and that the pursuit of this interest involved the exploitation of the working class. If the 'bureaucracy' is made up of vertical ministerial institutions, it would have to be demonstrated that it could protect itself against the Party and particularly against control by the Party Secretariat. Little empirical evidence has been collected to show the truth or falsity of these propositions.

It also seems doubtful whether the 'state-capitalist' theory succeeds in reconciling bureaucratic control with Marxist theory. Two main objections may be raised. First, the unity of the bureaucratic groups again is not adequately demonstrated. According to Schachtman, the new ruling class includes managers and Party Secretaries at the factory level whose interests have become fused together in a way 'similar though not quite identical with historic fusings into one class of different social strata' (1962, p. 71). However, the decisions over production may be taken at a much higher level than the factory, and it is not at all obvious that the economic interests of factory managers and the political interests of political chiefs of Party and government are necessarily congruent. Again, if the theory is based on the assumption of the merging of interests of owners (the Party in the sense that it defines and safeguards relations to the means of production) and managers (the state administration), then this, too, must be demonstrated. While Schachtman's paper 'Russia's new ruling class' was originally published in 1942 (republished 1966), it refers to the conditions of the 1930s. But at that time, as well as in the present, Party and state administrations have been separate. Indeed, Djilas's 'new class' theory sees the Party as the incumbent institution of class rule: 'The new ownership is not the same as the political government, but is created and aided by that government. The use, enjoyment and distribution of property is the privilege of the party and the party's top men' (1966, p. 65).

A second objection to state-capitalist theory which might be made concerns the notion of an ownership nexus between state property and the bureaucracy. However much control they have over Soviet production enterprises, managers and administrators can neither dispose of their assets for their private good, nor can their children have any exclusive rights to nationalised property. Kuron and Modzelewski avoid this issue by a 'party élite' explanation: the party élite is 'at one and the same time also the power élite; all decisions relating to state power are made by it ... by exercising state power, the party élite has at its disposal all the nationalized means of production ...' (1968, p. 7). They assume that the Party and government apparatus are fused and thus ignore the differentiation that takes place between these groupings (as noted above in Chapter 4). Their argument that property is owned collectively by 'the bureaucracy' cannot account satisfactorily for change and conflict within the system, such as was demonstrated by the course of events in 1956 and 1970–1 in Poland or in 1968 in Czechoslovakia, which reflected the rise and fall of distinct groups within the (unitary) 'central political bureaucracy'. The point is well made by Wesolowski (1979) that a Marxist analysis of society in terms of élite rule must locate such power in the context of class structure, in terms of ownership relations and the end use of surplus product. Many critical Marxists adopt a democratic radical critique in the manner of Wright Mills's analysis of American society.

A third objection to the state-capitalist theory lies in the field of the political economy (rather than political sociology) of state socialism. A crucial component of the Marxist analysis of capitalism lies in the fact that the extraction of surplus value is dependent on the competition of capitals which is a dynamic of the capitalist mode of production. State-capitalist theorists do not demonstrate how 'direct military competition' or an 'arms economy' is a necessary part of the economy of state socialism leading to the formation of social classes. It is not clear to me why defence expenditure should not be conceived of simply as a response to an external threat. It is true that defence expenditure involves the extraction of surplus labour from the producers. This in itself, however, is not evidence of class exploitation. Marx himself explicitly recognised that all, except the most primitive, forms of social production need to extract a surplus. Even under ideal Communist conditions the extraction of surplus would be necessary for the expansion of the process of reproduction, for the renewal of capital as well as for the maintenance of non-productive labour (e.g. pensioners, children). (See Marx, 1962, ch. XLIX.) Under capitalism the extraction of surplus labour 'assumes an antagonistic form and is supplemented by the complete idleness of a stratum of society' (ibid., p. 799). There may indeed be forms of what Bahro (1978, pp. 146–7) calls 'subalternity', political authority and domination (such as men over women). But this does not add up to what Marx meant by antagonistic class relations (see further discussion below, pp. 140–6). The existence of bureaucratic, intellectual, administrative and executive strata are also not analogous to the parasitical role of the capitalist shareholder envisaged by Marx.

These theories, stemming from a Marxist origin, emphasise objective class position: the incumbents of certain positions have rights and power which confer economic, social and political privileges, even though the leading members of the bureaucracy may not be conscious of their class position. Djilas says that the new class is 'the least deluded and least conscious of itself' and that the Communist 'is not conscious of the fact that he belongs to a new class, for he does not take into account the special privileges he enjoys . . . He cannot see that . . . he belongs to a special social category: *the ownership class*' (1966, pp. 64–5).

Conversely, the exploited may not necessarily be aware of the rulers' 'ownership' privileges, although writers such as Djilas take the view that at some stage a revolution will be necessary to overthrow the 'new class'. Here, again, we encounter a difficulty: how and in what circumstances could a revolutionary working class arise? Trotsky himself saw a possibility that the Party 'enriched with the attributes of old Bolshevism' itself might overthrow the bureaucracy and would restore democracy in the unions and freedom to political parties (1945, p. 252). None of the theorists of the 'bureaucratic class' mentioned solves this problem, although some contemporary exponents of the state-capitalist theory do not look to the Leninist form of party organisation as a means of regeneration but rather place their hopes on initiative coming from workers' control at the lowest levels. Cliff, for instance, sees the events of the Hungarian revolution as 'the great rehearsal' for such a revolution: 'The workers spontaneously created a system of workers' councils which became the leaders of the entire people in revolt. These workers' councils which sprang up in different parts of the country immediately faced the task of federating. They were groping towards the establishment of a Soviet Republic' (1964, p. 347). (See also the detailed proposals for workers' control and workers' political parties in Kuron and Modzelewski, 1968, pp. 59–68.)

In the 1950s and 1960s there was little evidence to suggest that the working class, as such, had developed a consciousness let alone any political organisation which would form a basis for revolt against the ruling classes in the socialist societies we are considering. In Hungary in 1956, the liberation movement had a national rather than a class character. In Czechoslovakia, it will be remembered, the liberal measures of 1968 were introduced by the Communist Party and though they would have weakened Party control over the ministries and ministerial control over industrial enterprises, they would have strengthened, rather than weakened, the power of managers. Indeed, the Soviet criticism of the intended changes in the Czech power structure was precisely that the Party would lose control over the managerial social strata. (This was in addition to opposition to other policies on foreign affairs and the media.) From the greater freedom and initiative of industrial managers and the destruction of the central apparatus of central planning in favour of the market it was feared that a way would be paved for a free-enterprise economy not unlike that in Western Europe. According to this viewpoint, workers' councils would not be effective mechanisms of control because the market would largely determine production and distribution policy, and workers' delegates to the councils would, at best, be able only to gain for the rank and file a greater share in the economic surplus of the firm. This, in turn, might have the undesirable effect of giving them a shareholders' mentality. (See also Riddell's criticisms of workers' control in Yugoslavia – 1968, p. 58.)

The tensions in Poland in the 1970s and early 1980s do evidence greater unrest and spontaneous opposition to the government by the manual working class. Strikes and demands for independent trade unions spearheaded by shipyard workers brought home the grievances of groups of workers who thought that their interests were not represented or heeded by the government. This activity may bring into question a major assumption made by Wesolowski (discussed above in Chapter 1) that state-socialist society is legitimate because it operates in the interest of the working class (1979, p. 122). While it must be conceded that it is not necessary for the members of a class to 'possess' the state (industrial and financial capitalists do not sit in control of the capitalist state), it may be questioned as to whether the present organisation of state-socialist society, with political leadership in the hands of the Communist Party, does lead to an unequivocal identity of class interests and political power. The movement in Poland for greater workers' power, however, is not simply a revolutionary insurgent communist movement as postulated by Cliff. In addition to economistic demands, claims are made for changing the balance of power within the state by ensuring rights to strike (with full pay [sic]) and to organise independent trade unions. (See the twenty-one demands of Gdansk strikers, *Soviet Studies*, vol. 23, 1981, pp. 222–3.)

The setting up of free trade unions might divert resources from investment to consumption and weaken the state's ability to plan comprehensively. The movement also includes many liberal, bourgeois, chauvinistic and religious elements (see Ticktin, 1981, pp. 69–71). In Poland, the very poor performance of the economy is exacerbated by the comparisons made with the capitalist Baltic states and with expatriate Poles. The legitimacy of the state is more under question where discord between the various élite interests has implications for the global strategy of the USSR; hence a policy which appears to be 'Polish' and anti-Russian has the effect of rallying non-élite groups, while identification with Soviet policies brings national sovereignty into question. Also the legitimacy of the Polish state, the sovereignty of the Party, is more in question in Poland than in the USSR.

The final criticism which may be levelled at the bureaucratic collectivist and the state-capitalist theories is that even if one can show that a particular social stratum takes effective decisions over the means of production, it does not necessarily follow that the incumbents are acting in their own class interests to exploit the masses. It is possible that other social forces play an important role in the decisions of the leadership. The bureaucracy is subject to rules or laws and the broader values and beliefs which give the system its legitimacy constitute a framework within which the élite must operate. Here the idea of the economic plan and the notion of the building of communism are integrative mechanisms which bind the élites as much as the non-élites. The internal growth of all societies following the Soviet model and their dynamism are the result of particular values which have set limits on the monopolisation of power by the political élites. Ticktin and Meikle's notion that state-socialist societies are 'moribund' is open to question; and, while the rate of economic growth has declined, in the 1970s and 1980s the development and spread of the 'Soviet model' to Asia and Africa throws doubts on the idea that such societies represent a historical *cul-de-sac*. It must be conceded, however, that the hegemony of political power asserted by the Communist Party leadership in the early period of the revolution may act as a constraint on the legitimate articulation of interests by the masses as socialist societies mature. The role of the political bureaucracy has been developed by non-Marxist critics of socialist societies and it is to these that we now turn.

NEO-WEBERIAN CRITIQUE

Frank Parkin has remarked that the attempts by contemporary Marxists to make Marxism relevant to the conditions of capitalist societies in the late twentieth century have led them to adopt concepts derived from bourgeois sociology and analysis alien to classical Marxism. 'Inside every neo-Marxist there seems to be a Weberian struggling to get out' (1979, p. 25). Nowhere is this more true than in the analysis of state-socialist societies. Many writers (quite contrary to Marx's intentions) replace ownership with control and see division of labour, particularly authority inhering in positions of control, as constituting the basis of political power. Zukin (1978) is a contemporary example of one who seeks legitimacy in a Marxist style while simultaneously removing the foundations of a Marxist analysis of class: 'The concept of class must move away from reliance on a straightforward criterion of "relations to the means of production" and towards an understanding of the role of extra-economic factors in creating and maintaining class relations.' The gist of the remarks made in the previous section is that such analyses do contain an element of truth – but that they are not Marxist analyses. Parkin emphasises the importance of moving away from such a position and he considers the Weberian notion of 'social closure' to be more apt and applicable to state-socialist societies than the Marxist concept of social classes.

By 'social closure' is meant the process by which a wide range of social groups (class, occupational, gender, racial, religious) seek to maximise their own rewards and to exclude access from 'subordinate outsiders' to 'resources and opportunities' (1979, p. 44). Exploitation, for Parkin, is the 'nexus between classes or other collectivities that stand in a relationship of dominance and subordination on *whatever* social basis' (p. 46). The notion of ownership is retained but widened to embody any minority having access to property (in the sense of capital) which leads to

> important consequences for the life chances and social condition of the excluded . . . Once property is conceptualised as a form of exclusionary social closure there is no need to become entangled in semantic debates over whether or not

workers in socialist states are 'really' exploited. The relevant question is not whether surplus extraction occurs but whether the state confers rights upon a limited circle of eligibles to deny access to the 'means of life and labour' to the rest of the community. (p. 53)

This approach shares with Giddens a much wider definition of exploitation than that of Marxists. As Giddens has put it: exploitation is 'any socially conditioned form of asymmetrical production of life chances' (1973, p. 130) which may include cultural, educational, gender, occupational and class forms of differentiation.

Critics, including Parkin, interpret the persistence of authority relations in quite a different way to Wesolowski, mentioned above (see Chapter 1). They consider that, while not being members of a bourgeois capitalist class, those holding positions of authority have power, status and enjoy a greater share in the consumption of valued commodities. Such powers of exclusion over income, status and power are not transitional but structural and reflect the fact that society is in a state of permanent tension, of 'unrelieved distributive struggle' (1979, p. 112). Parkin then analyses industrial rather than capitalist or socialist society and agrees with neo-Marxists that 'the manager is capital personified' under monopoly capitalism and state socialism (p. 53).

Alvin Gouldner pours new wine into this convergence bottle. For him the late twentieth century heralds the 'new class' of intellectuals and technical intelligentsia. At root the 'new class' grows out of the changing occupational structure in the shape of the large group of educated professional and technical white-collar strata which is ideologically bound by the ethics of professionalism, given cohesion by its distinctive language and 'culture of discourse' and politically united – 'the "vanguard" party expresses the modernising and élite ambitions of the New Class . . .' (1979, p. 5). The distinctive feature of the 'new class', which is in power in state-socialist societies is its 'cultural or human capital' (p. 8), hence Gouldner replaces orthodox Marxist ownership of the means of production by the conception of 'a new *cultural* bourgeoisie . . . [with] control over valuable cultures' (p. 21). For Gouldner, the 'new class' is a 'flawed universal class': it is at once 'the most progressive force' in modern society and a 'center of human emancipation', but it does not herald the end of domination – for the 'New Class is also the nucleus of a *new* hierarchy and the élite of a new form of cultural capital' (p. 83).

Konrad and Szelenyi develop the 'new class' thesis and apply it with important amendments to the structure of East European societies. These writers view the 'new class' not as the embodiment of reason but as the instruments of a 'new system of oppression and exploitation of the working class . . .' (1979, p. xiii). Under state socialism, the intelligentsia, widely defined to include all persons with higher qualifications, forms a dominant class. Szelenyi and Konrad correctly observe that if the analysis of class is dependent on market conditions then 'we must abandon the concept of class in dealing with socialist societies, which are fundamentally redistributive in character' (p. 45).

Konrad and Szelenyi see the class power of the 'new class' as being derived from its control of the redistribution of surplus product: it confers rights on itself to the exclusion of the rest of the community, its goal being to maximise the extraction of surplus (created by the working class) and to use it to expand the investment goods industry (pp. 154–5). Unlike under capitalism, it has no foe in the form of a bourgeoisie which legitimates its appropriation of surplus through ownership. Also, intellectuals in Eastern Europe are strengthened by the bureaucracy and the police: one might define the ruling élites – analogous to the definition of C. Wright Mills – as being composed of a united triumvirate of Party ideologue, policeman and technocrat (p. 148). These writers, together with Bahro, Parkin and Giddens see the political élites in the form of the Party and state bureaucracies as being exploitative. 'The ruling élite is the supreme guardian of the ethos of rational redistribution . . . its planning logic and social and economic policies are diametrically opposed to the interests of the workers' (Konrad and Szelenyi, 1979, p. 230). For Giddens, state-socialist societies have created a 'system of political domination which has altered the character of social exploitation rather than in any sense diminishing it' (1973, p. 294).

With the exception of Parkin (1979), who does not envision

any future without social closure and therefore considers social relations to be in permanent tension, all these writers advocate change of an essentially political kind within the parameters of the present arrangements of property. Giddens following Cliff notes a tendency for a 'resurgence of demands for the extension of workers' management – and thus a "counter-communism" based upon ideas of localized cooperatives and genuine worker participation in the exercise of authority in industry' (1973, p. 251). Konrad and Szelenyi echo the Marxist ideal by postulating an alternative society based on the legitimacy of those who create surplus product and look to a return to collective bargaining cooperatives and workers' self-management.

Bahro (1978) is more complex. He views the hierarchical structure of the division of labour as being at the root of the various forms of alienation in state-socialist society. He seeks a revitalisation of the human being who must become active, rather than passive, 'conscious' rather than 'manipulated' and 'universal' rather than 'one-dimensional'. He seeks, then, a revitalisation of the human spirit through a cultural revolution which will invigorate the Party.

There can be no doubt that the occupational structure of industrial societies calls for an analysis putting the new white-collar professions and semi-professions at the centre of its analysis: even in a Leninist sense, the technician/technologist now replaces the skilled metalworkers as the most technically advanced part of the working class. Yet one must question whether the evidence would justify giving the intellectuals/ intelligentsia a similar role as an historical force as the bourgeoisie. The internal differentiation of so wide an occupational stratum as 'intellectuals' (including managers, technologists, welfare workers, teachers and the traditional intelligentsia of creative writer and social critic) is great and the evidence we have considered does not confirm the view that they share a common world view. True, the advocates of the 'new class' thesis would argue that it is internally differentiated – but have these groups sufficient in common to form a common class interest? The character of the political leadership representing the intellectuals as a class in state socialism is even more open to question. Even with the caveats offered by Konrad and Szelenyi, it seems to be far from convincing to suggest that intellectuals, ideologues and police may be considered as a unitary power bloc. Rather one might hypothesise many manifest cleavages between these strata – on such issues as the role of the market, on military intervention in Afghanistan or Czechoslovakia, on relations with China. Perhaps the truth of the matter is that the new white-collar groups have greater potential for political action and control than hitherto, but that political decisions may be influenced more by traditional interests (Party, police and military) than the theorists of the 'new class' would concede. The recognition of the 'potential' for power is commonplace – the slaves of antiquity, the industrial worker under capitalism, all have 'potential' for seizing power. The question to be addressed is whether there is a likelihood of such potential being translated into the actual.

Yet Parkin is certainly correct to complain that Marxists tend to conflate all kinds of conflict into one type of class conflict. One must acknowledge that authority may be misused and that the control of decision-making and executives by those subject to them is not developed in socialist states. Staniszkis (1979), a Polish critic and adviser to Solidarity takes up this point. She argues that the institutional system may create an 'inert balance'. 'Defensive mechanisms' block the decisions made at the 'steering centre' (government and Party). Staniszkis assumes that there are conflicts of interests between various actors in the social system: those who are subject to new initiatives by the centre devise counter-strategies to hinder them. These blockages create dysfunctions in the operation of the economy and in the effectiveness of the social system. Interests in socialist society do not always coincide and may be manifested in severe conflicts, especially when the economy is mismanaged. While Staniszkis sees her work as being Marxist in orientation, it seems to me to owe a greater debt to non-Marxist theories of bureaucracy and organisation than to the works of Marx. Along these lines Hirszowicz (1980) has placed the concept of 'bureaucracy' at the centre of the analysis of socialist society. She points out that the institutional forms of socialist states are defended by the political élites and do not change to meet social and economic needs. The 'dysfunctional' aspects of bureaucracy include: 'the excessive growth of rules and regulations . . . The inevitable rigidity of the organisational structures . . . Overcentralisation as the cause of unavoidable delays in decision-making on issues that require prompt and effective solutions . . . Excessive time and effort spent on co-ordinating activities . . . The displacement of goals due to the difficulties of harmonising organisational inducements with the nature of the tasks to be performed . . . Defence mechanisms of functionaries against clients, customers and outsiders' (Hirszowicz, 1980, p. 135). Political change, then, has an 'explosive character' as non-élite groups confront the 'establishment' to further 'rational change' (ibid., p. 132).

One serious problem lies in the political sphere and this has been highlighted in 1981 by the demands of Polish Communist Party members for greater participation in decision-making (see *Labour Focus on Eastern Europe*, Winter–Spring, 1981, pp. 50–4). Here one may distinguish between input participation and output participation. Input participation is concerned with the way in which individuals or groups actively shape or influence decisions or policies, whereas output participation seeks to mobilise people to carry out orders and instructions. The traditional Soviet form of participation has strongly developed such 'output' mechanisms in the shape of trade unions, Soviets, street committees and election campaigns (see Friedgut, 1979); the Party has also been a 'conveyor belt' of such decisions. In the period of the early development of socialist society a premium was correctly placed on mobilisation policies, of ensuring participation of uprooted people in a society undergoing industrialisation. In a more socially and economically developed society, however, greater input participation is necessary to resolve the many conflicts of interest that may arise, but the Party leadership is often reluctant to allow these interests to develop as it fears that its own legitimacy will be undermined. This results in the greater politicisation of life as authoritative mechanisms for conflict resolution cannot be institutionalised. At the root of the 'bureaucratisation' of processes and relationships in state-socialist societies is a lack of genuine 'input' participation. Party activists in Poland in the 'anti-*apparat* movement' in 1981 have called for the democratisation of the Party along the lines of accountability, recall and genuine election of all officials and the formation of interest factions in the Party (*Labour Focus on Eastern Europe*, loc. cit., p. 51).

Dissident writers often call for the replacement (or severe modification) of the system of central planning and control. In their stead they advocate 'free collective bargaining', greater reliance on the market and workers' self-management. Ironically, perhaps, socialists in the West view dependence on such processes of market exchange under capitalism with distaste and it is also possible that if given free play, they will also lead in socialist states to greater individualism, to competitiveness between different sections of the working class, to a reduction of the state's ability to promote equality by curbing powerful bargaining interests, by developing backward areas and by protecting weakly organised groups. Collective bargaining and a reliance on the market may enhance freedom of action but it may exact a price in terms of the reduction of equality. (On such tendencies in Yugoslavia, see D. Lane, 1976, pp. 146–53.) Hence much of the acclaim for the independent labour movement in Poland must be seen in liberal and democratic terms.

THE TOTALITARIAN-MASS MODEL

This emphasis on the 'political' component has led to the formation of a school of thinkers which emphasises the role of the state and the absence of freedom under socialism. While the ruling and/or neo-Marxist theory has been accepted by many 'new class' writers outside the official Communist Parties yet another conflict theory has wide currency – that of totalitarianism. Like Marxism, the totalitarian model is not simply confined to the study of social class and stratification, but sets out to show how the domination of the political system over society takes place after communist (or fascist) types of political parties have seized power. But unlike neo-Marxism, the advocates of this model have little time for class theory or any of the concepts noted above. The most succinct definition is that of Friedrich (Friedrich, Curtis and Barber, 1969, p. 136) who defines totalitarianism as 'a system of autocratic rule for realising totalist intentions under modern technical conditions'. Friedrich and

Brzezinski (1966, pp. 22–3) identify eight traits of a totalitarian system. The six main characteristics are: an official ideology, a single mass party typically led by one man, a system of terroristic Party control, a technologically conditioned near-monopoly of control of the effective mass media and means of armed combat, central control, and direction of the entire economy; two other, though less important, traits are also suggested: administrative control of justice, and expansion. In the present context we may define the social structure of totalitarian society as consisting basically of a dichotomous and exploitative set of social relations between ruling élite and an amorphous, socially ineffective mass.

The best-known sociological discussions of totalitarianism which hail from the time of the Cold War are those of Kornhauser (1960), Aron (1950) and Arendt (1958). Aron's argument is quite ingenious. He attempts to combine Marx's class analysis and Pareto's élite theory. He concludes that a classless society is achieved under totalitarianism; but unlike the kind of classless society envisaged by Marx, it is one in which an élite rules a fragmented mass. The unitary élite is made up of a

> small number of men who in practice run the industrial undertakings, command the army, decide what proportion of the national resources should be allocated to savings and investment and fix scales of remuneration. The minority has infinitely more power than the political rulers in a democratic society, because both political and economic power are concentrated in their hands . . . The unified élite has absolute and unbounded power . . . A classless society leaves the mass of the population without any possible means of defence against the élite. (1950, pt 2, p. 131)

Totalitarianism, argues Aron, solves the problem of conflict in modern society by reducing society to 'obedience' rather than, as Marx suggested, by general liberation. The élite must be monistic because otherwise all economic and political power will not be concentrated at one source which is a necessary condition for planning in a collectivised economy. Aron accepts the view that Soviet society is classless in Marxist terms: 'every member of the population has his share in ownership, since the means of production belong to the community, and everyone is a wage-earner because all incomes are derived from work'. Conflict between groups does not exist because of the strength of the unitary élite and the weakness of group cohesion among the masses.

The nature of totalitarian society has been described in detail by Arendt who holds that, unlike a society characterised by a hierarchical ranking of strata or even by a polarised system of classes, a mass society is composed of individuals who lack consciousness of common interest and who, therefore, cannot be integrated into interest groups. Arendt argues that, in Soviet society, Stalin 'fabricated an atomized and structureless "mass"' (1958, pp. 318–23; see also Feldmesser, 1966, p. 533). It follows from the theory of 'mass society' that a characteristic of a totalitarian social structure is its lack of structure which is deliberately promoted by the ruling élite. Arendt's view is that in Soviet Russia, group formations among the non-élites had to be abolished, otherwise they would have developed interests hostile to the ruling élite. The structure of intermediate groups (that is, those between the family and the state) in totalitarian theory has been somewhat refined by Kornhauser, who argues that not only are the intermediate groups weak, but that they are also 'inclusive', that is, controlled by the ruling élite through 'front' organisations. The ruling élite itself is made up of the top echelons of the Party which has developed channels of direct access to the otherwise unorganised individuals in the society. Thus a Soviet-type society is mainly distinguished from a modern capitalist one by the fact that in the former a unified political ruling élite determines the shape of the social system, whereas in the latter there exists a number of competing élites who represent autonomous social groupings with different interests.

Most of the serious analyses of totalitarianism have been carried out by political scientists rather than sociologists and, in general, they have been concerned to define the structure of the ruling élite. (See, for example, Friedrich and Brzezinski, 1966; and Friedrich, Curtis and Barber, 1969.) These books are devoted to the analysis of the socio-political system rather than to inequality and social stratification as such. (For a critical appraisal see Rigby, 1972.) Recent thinking has tended to question the idea of the monistic nature of the élite by showing that at the apex of power a number of specific interests may impinge upon the ruling apparatus (Meyer, 1964; Skilling and Griffiths, 1971; Hough, 1977; Bialer, 1980*b*). Meyer, for example, cites the interests of such groups as industrial and administrative executives, military and security officers, leading scientists and other highly placed opinion-makers. This line of thought is an attempt to account for conflict within the ruling élite while, at the same time, preserving the basic conception of its unity against the non-élite – the mass. Meyer also considers the role played by social mobility in providing the recruitment of 'new blood' into the élite from the mass. This process not only helps to prevent the formation of a group consciousness among the subordinate population but gives some credence to a value system which is based on notions of merit and achievement.

It would take us outside the bounds of this short book to discuss in detail the deficiencies of the totalitarian model, but some of the more important defects may be noted here. First, as we saw above when criticising the neo-Marxist theories, insufficient attention is given to the content of the ideology which helps determine the path which social change should take. As was pointed out in Chapter 1, terror was utilised by the Bolsheviks in the early period of Soviet rule against the class enemies of the regime and industrialisation was not simply adopted by the political leadership to help 'massify' the population, but was in keeping with their views of class war, and cannot be abstracted from a consideration of Marxist-Leninist theory.

Secondly, it seems most unlikely that any society can remain in a state of perpetual terror or 'massification'. Personal security, the fulfilment of certain minimum expectations about one's career, living standards and the education of one's children would seem to be a minimum condition of social life in modern society. Indeed, Friedrich in 1969 conceded that physical terror has been replaced by psychic terror and that a social consensus had developed. Also, the totalitarian model is an 'immanent' or static analysis ignoring the causes of changes in the structure of society through time. The point need not be laboured again that in state-socialist society urbanisation and industrialisation have had important consequences for the occupational and social structure. In the advanced phase of the development of these societies, professional and regional interests are articulated and play an important part in the political process. (I have described elsewhere the role of different groups in the Soviet political process – D. Lane, 1978, ch. 8. See also Skilling and Griffiths, 1971, and Hough, 1976.)

Thirdly, and as Hough has pointed out, there is a methodological bias and conservative ideology entwined in this school's approach. The institutions of state-socialist societies are compared with the ideals of the ways that American democracy should work. The actual processes of state socialism involve – asserts Hough – wide-ranging participation and the Party, rather than being a 'priesthood that stands outside of society', has incorporated 'virtually all societal interests' (1977, p. 9). The system is one of 'institutional pluralism' and has a basic legitimacy.

The totalitarian model may be more appropriate to the period of rapid state-led industrialisation than to the more mature industrial society. Totalitarianism stresses the coercive role of political élites, the importance of their control of mass communications and the means of violence, while also giving a prominent place to the rapid social mobility and the purges of the 1930s. Applied to the present day, it is less useful. State-socialist societies are socially hierarchical and stratified. But, and despite Hough's protestations, totalitarianism does point to some of the political inadequacies of state-socialist societies. In a mature socialist society, after all, one would not expect to find excessive restraints on communication, or the lack of civil freedoms, such as the right to travel abroad, criticised by writers such as Medvedev (1971) and the Solidarity and Party activists in Poland. These points are taken up by socialist writers as well as conservative ones. While Western states have many inadequacies in terms of democratic participation, governments are answerable to their citizens and political leaders may lose their positions through public pressure and a regularised process of public reselection which is not the case in the USSR or any other socialist state.

Developments in Poland and Czechoslovakia have illustrated the indirect pressure of interest groups and public dissatisfaction; in 1981 the institutionalisation of conflict in Poland was further enhanced by the open election of the Politburo by the Central Committee of the Party. One might again turn Hough on his head by arguing that similarities between the political processes of the USA and the USSR do not amount to very much if one conceives of the American system as being essentially élitist and exercising political power through the prevention of the articulation and dissemination of fundamental (socialist) criticism. One similarity that the countries do not share is the scope of government. The absence of private capital is both a constraint over the individual's freedom which is understandably disliked by bourgeois thinkers, but it also gives rise to the possibility of industrial democracy, of public accountability and control, of the utilisation of resources to achieve equality, and this is why socialists view such control in a different light from liberals. Hence the claims for 'freedom' against 'equality' advocated by neo-conservatives such as Connor (1979) are themselves posed in an abstract way, because they overlook the limitations which are imposed on 'freedom' by the class structure and political domination of the state in Western capitalist countries and the extent to which privilege and poverty are structurally reproduced. Perhaps the kernel of truth in the approach of Friedrich would be to classify state-socialist society at one end of the continuum with high government control, and the USA at the other with low government control, and to leave out the political values as to whether this is a good or bad thing. One other methodological inadequacy is that the totalitarian approach, like that of the 'ruling élite' is not located in a Marxist theory of class structure. While Marxist writers, and particularly those apologising for existing state-socialist societies, ignore or minimise antagonism between the masses and the ruling élite, 'conflict theorists' likewise ignore or minimise the importance of the class structure.

6 Conclusions

In the foregoing chapters we have seen that the Bolshevik Revolution succeeded in changing the fundamental relations of power and property but that it has not subsequently created a society ensuring the equality of men, one in which social stratification – in a relational and distributive sense – is absent. There are four reasons why social inequality persists in the USSR and in states modelled on her; it has been perpetuated, first, by property relations, secondly, by the system of political power, thirdly, by the division of labour and fourthly, by the human nuclear family. Let us consider each and then turn to outline the major social cleavages in state-socialist society.

The concept of class with which Marx, Lenin, Trotsky and Stalin are associated takes as its starting-point the relations of social groups to the ownership of the means of production. Whereas the inalienable right of man to possess private property was proclaimed by the French Revolution, the Russian Revolution of October 1917 sought to destroy the human bondage to private property. In both revolutions class rights played a large and important part – they were a catalyst of the desires for social change of particular social groups. After the Bolshevik Revolution, the concept of class struggle became a dominating factor in the transformation of Russia. The ideology of historical materialism in which class rights prominently figured severely limited the possibilities of social action which were open to Russia's leaders, and it became the basis of a value system on which the actual structure of social relations in the USSR and the other East European societies has been built and judged. The incumbents of power in the USSR, those who defend it as a socialist society, are committed to a view of the world which gives to the private ownership of property primacy in the determination of social relations. But ownership has both legal and social connotations. In a legal sense it gives exclusive rights to the possessor of an object to dispose of it or enjoy it. But the rules or legal charter of a society may not coincide with actual social relations. Certain groups (for example, government ministers and their subordinates such as factory directors) may, in fact, have certain rights over objects which are not given legal recognition, and this makes formal legal interpretations unrealistic. Hence many writers, and not only the 'official' Soviet ones, have considered ownership and the classes arising from it in a mechanical way. While large-scale private property has been largely abolished, property is not owned in common in state-socialist societies. In addition to private ownership in agriculture (the produce of personal plots), the notion of property is perpetuated by institutional control of wealth (for example, by the state bank, ministries and institutions). These factors not only influence the individual's consciousness of property but give rights and privileges to those who are able to control property. The implications of such ownership forms are twofold. On the one hand, the incumbents of power positions (those with authority) do not form an ownership class which can be understood in classical Marxist terms. Assets are not disposed of through families in state-socialist societies. Government ministers and directors of factories do not pass on rights over ministries or factories to their sons as do many capitalists in Western societies. Also, those with control over property giving them privileges in the distribution of rewards are not conscious of their property rights and there is no ideological foundation to legitimate their group power: therefore they do not form a ruling class as defined by Marx. This difference represents a break between the system of stratification in Western advanced capitalist societies and those of the Soviet type. On the other hand, societies arranged on the model of the USSR are not 'socialist' in the way in which classical Marxists conceived of such a social system. A necessary condition for a socialist type of society is not only the abolition of proprietory classes, but also the development of productive forces to a stage higher than that allowed by the fetters of capitalist property relations. However, most of the societies of Eastern Europe which we have considered have been characterised by a relatively under-developed industrial structure, being at the time of the Communist seizure of power nowhere near the level of that of the advanced states of Western Europe and the USA. Thus it is not surprising that with the development of these states the pattern of social relations which they exhibit is not, in general, qualitatively different from that of capitalist societies and is unlikely to be so until the capacity of the productive forces has surpassed those of the advanced capitalist societies of the West. Under the conditions inherited by the Communists in Eastern Europe, the bourgeoisie's traditional task of capital formation involving urbanisation and industrialisation became that of the state which shaped to some extent the particular pattern of social stratification.

We have seen that the state had an impact on the group structure of East European societies: put simply, political power did not grow out of the group structure; it created a group structure. The predominantly agrarian societies of Eastern Europe have been industrialised by the political élites, and from such processes have followed changes in the number and size of occupational groups and in the distribution of income. This social transformation function of the state must not be exaggerated. It is not true to say that '. . . the system of inequality that we call social stratification is only a secondary consequence of the social structure of power' (Dahrendorf, 1969, p. 38). Certain forms of social distinction are independent of, rather than determined by, the system of political power. Those with the power to coerce other men (say, party officials or bureaucrats) do not always have high evaluation in terms of honour. The 'official charter' describes the urban working class as the legitimate bearer of socialist virtue and power but, in practice, the working class is stratified. The urban intelligentsia occupy positions of power (in the Party and government) and those of social honour (the professions), whereas the manual working class has much less power, income and honour. Study of the changing pattern of income differentials brings out the ways political ideological goals have been modified when under stress from adaptive economic pressures. The early policies of the Communist Party which aimed at levelling out incomes generally have not been long lasting because the constraints of economic and technical efficiency have required wider differentials. The evidence presented in this text showing similarities between capitalist and state-socialist societies concerning differential access to education, and the evaluation of the status of occupations, seems overwhelming and conclusive. These facts suggest that the political élites have been unable, in some respects, to shape the system of social stratification to their own specifications, and that they have been confronted with other social forces and institutions which have a certain autonomy. Conflict, then, is a feature of state-socialist society as it is of capitalist: the bureaucratic system is not a homogenous behavioural system, is not a unitary bureaucracy 'writ large', but is subject to internal interest formulation – the centre (in the form of the government or Party leadership) is subject to dissent and obstruction from those below. Guiding or organising society from the centre presents bureaucratic problems of a high order and these form the basis of many of the political disjunctions of state socialism. Occupation, gender, age, ethnic origin, bureaucratic position, Party and religious allegiance generate social and political interests which are manifested in conflicts between various groups in the controlling function and also for the distribution of resources. However, such relational and distributive inequality should not be conflated into a Marxist class conflict paradigm: power inheres in bureaucratic position, and interest may be derived from a variety of material and ideal sources. While the origins of the system of social stratification are to be found in the political order, after a revolutionary change many patterns of inequality come to approximate to the social stratification systems of other industrial societies. Particularly important in this respect are the impact of the division of labour and the functions performed by the family.

Social relations in modern industrial society are specialised and specific; there is a highly developed division of labour. The economic division of labour gives some men (few women) the creative tasks, those of planning and ordering the work of others; but the majority do the intellectually less exacting and routine jobs. The occupations of persons profoundly influence the esteem in which other people hold them and affect the way of life they follow. The intrinsic satisfaction of creative and executive jobs is greater than that of unskilled. The job itself develops or hinders other individual capacities: those with creative positions are able to exploit their intelligence, they become skilled in manipulating symbols, machines and other men. They form social groups and mix with others of a similar intellectual background. Similarly, the occupation of the unskilled also influences their ranking in terms of power and honour. Hence, as long as the economic organisation of society calls for the division of labour, status differentials are likely to continue.

Two points may be made here about the practical possibilities of creating an equalitarian society. First, one may reject the argument of those egalitarians who claim that all jobs are equally 'necessary' in a society and that therefore all should be equal in status. While any job may be 'necessary' if it has a social purpose, not all jobs may be performed equally well by each individual and some form of role differentiation is necessary to promote the effective use of resources through technical efficiency. Educational systems are structures whose *raison d'être* is to train some men for more complicated and specialised tasks and others to accept the less demanding and more routine. The former are given a near monopoly of certain skills and those with no skill or little skill are in a weak competitive position, whereas the skilled can much more easily perform unskilled jobs. At any given time, therefore, the indispensability of the highly skilled, as they are more difficult to substitute, is greater than that of the unskilled. Secondly, those with intellectual skills are able to influence political power, they are able to manipulate symbols and to justify distributional privileges. To some extent they may be able to maintain privileges which are quite unrelated to their scarcity and to manipulate other men to believe that their privileges are necessary for the society to function properly. The division of labour, then, has a certain 'objective' hierarchy built into it and also has a self-justifying mechanism. Even if the view that all contribute equally to the maintenance of a system is over-simple, the ability of the privileged groups to appropriate more than an equal share of the social product and to secure the compliance of the underprivileged to their superiority are based on the division of labour and will continue until it is no longer necessary. Thus attempts to 'introduce equality' by influencing social norms through the educational system are likely to have only limited effect unless accompanied by significant changes in the economic system (the mode of production).

Another source of inequality in state-socialist society is the nuclear family as an institution. Parents have an occupational role and status in society which under present arrangements significantly influence their children's access to the culture of that society. The inheritance of wealth has been restricted by the structural form of state-socialist society and has had the effect of making social position more dependent on achievement than ascription by family origin. But to a very great extent access to education, to the stock of knowledge of how the system works and to basic social and intellectual skills is still inherited through the family circle, thereby thwarting the equalitarian plans pursued by revolutionary leaders. During the periods of rapid industrialisation and social change which characterised the early period of Communist power in state-socialist society, the family was weakened and the social structure was in flux. After this period, and with the consolidation of Communist rule, the family has been strengthened and there has been a tendency to a less flexible system of social stratification. There are two reasons for the persistence of the nuclear family in a form similar to that of the capitalist West. First, it is an institution through which individuals may satisfy their own emotional demands: to give and to receive affection, to gratify regularly and without competition their sexual urges. It is also a mechanism which helps to integrate the social order. It ensures the care, maintenance and socialisation of children and, in so doing, it does not infringe upon the rights of the privileged. Thus the incumbents of positions of power and privilege find it useful both in their own interest and in the interest of society as a whole to strengthen the family. At the same time, the family perpetuates other more traditional attitudes which may be at variance with the values of the political élites. For instance, prejudice about the inferiority of woman and her 'proper' roles and about national and ethnic groups is passed on in the socialisation process which takes place in the family.

The major social divisions in state-socialist society are threefold. First, there are differences between the working class (both manual and non-manual) and the peasantry. The latter occupies an inferior position when compared to the working class in terms of income, access to power (Party), and social honour. Such differences are accounted for by the peasantry's greater attachment to private property and also by the peculiar values of Eastern European societies where peasants have historically constituted the most underprivileged and least honoured stratum. Secondly, there is a division between manual and non-manual labour. While income differentials sometimes mask such differences, there is a fairly well crystallised differentiation between those who work mainly with their hands and those who use their brains. This division is much less distinct on the borderline between unskilled non-manual and skilled manual, but is more definite at the upper levels between the 'socialist intelligentsia' with higher educational qualifications and the rest of the manual strata. This group is distinguished by high social honour, high income, more 'cultured' forms of consumption and by patterns of friendship and marriages. In the period of rapid industrialisation and political change it has been characterised by much recruitment from the manual strata, but with the slowdown of economic growth and with the greater stability of the political system, this feature becomes less distinctive and gives way to internal regeneration. The third main division in state-socialist society is between the political leadership which has its privilege grounded in political power and the technocratic and professional groups whose rights are based on technical and administrative knowledge. The ideals and values of socialist revolution have been associated with the former, but the Party's role in an industrial society has changed. A state-socialist society is, above all, a technical-administrative society, where man's social position is increasingly determined by education, qualifications and technical-administrative performance. The modern Party has co-opted into its ranks technical, intellectual and administrative personnel in large numbers, and also the popular base of the Party has expanded. But an important place in the political process must be given to Party officials, as such, who help define and steer the country according to their view of the national interest. The notion that a homogenous 'intellectual class' is in control must be rejected. While there is rivalry between groups at the top of the power structure, the élites also have a certain identity of interests to maintain their privileges against the non-élites. This balance is sometimes upset, as it was in Czechoslovakia when one element of the élite (the technical and cultural intelligentsia) utilised the non-élite to try to secure for itself greater power at the expense of another élite element (the Party bureaucrats). Thus the social foundation of politics in state-socialist society is neither one of ownership classes in the Marxist sense, nor of a ruling élite and fragmented mass as postulated by the theorists of totalitarianism. It is one of competing élites, operating in a bureaucratic structure, which are also subject to pressures arising from the masses – in Poland particularly, the working class.

We may conclude by saying that the system of social stratification in state-socialist society has peculiar features distinguishing it from those of advanced capitalist states. The limited individual private inheritance of wealth has eliminated ownership classes as known in capitalist societies, but it has put a premium on achievement as a mode by which inequality has been maintained and thus has given rise to institutional control over wealth enabling some men to have rights over property which others are denied. The ideology of state-socialist society has, perhaps marginally, enhanced the status of the workers as a social group, the extent of income differentials has been minimised and sex differences have been reduced.

But inequality is a characteristic of state-socialist society as it is of the capitalist: in a relational sense, there is inequality of control over wealth, inequality of political power, and in a distributive sense, there is inequality of income and inequality of status. The origins of such social stratification lie in the bureaucratic nature of political power, in the role structure created by the division of labour sanctioned by the educational system and perpetuated by the family. Such structural features give rise to a hierarchy in which some groups of men (and few women) have power, prestige and privilege while others lack them. Politically, and not without internal conflict, the privileged acquire the means to help maintain and to justify ideologically their advantage. Though social equality is a worthy ideal, the recent history of state-socialist society shows that it cannot be attained by the wishes of men independently of the economic structure of society. 'Men make their own history, but they do not make it

159

under circumstances chosen by themselves but under circumstances directly encountered, given and transmitted from the past' (Marx, 1958a, p. 247). Until such circumstances make differential ownership and control of property, the division of labour and the socialising influence of the nuclear family no longer necessary for the flourishing of industrial society, social inequality will remain a characteristic of the relations between men.

Present-day ·socialist societies are transitional: in Marxist terms, they are neither capitalist nor fully socialist. The class relations to the means of production are not capitalist in the sense that there is nothing equivalent to a bourgeois class, to the operation of an economy with its dynamic based on the production of exchange value. But the level of productive forces has not outstripped that of the capitalist world: state-socialist societies are still relatively underdeveloped compared with the capitalist West; shortages of goods lead to distribution problems which are solved in the fashion of bourgeois society – there being unequal distribution of rewards (according to one's work). We have seen that the superstructure of socialist states includes many incongruities: there is unequal participation in the state; women are underprivileged. The relationships and forms of distribution we have discussed are certainly not 'socialist' in an ideal sense. One must bear in mind the fact that state-socialist societies have progressed very rapidly from being backward societies and they have inherited a traditional and non-democratic culture, in so doing they bear the hallmark of their own history, of their autocratic and feudal past.

References

Aage, H. (1981), 'The significance of wage differentials for the allocation of labour in the Soviet Union', unpublished paper (Birmingham: Centre for Russian and East European Studies).

Aganbegyan, A. G., Osipov, G. V. and Shubkin, V. N. (1966), *Kolichestvennye metody v sotsiologii* (Moscow).

Allworth, E. (1980), *Ethnic Russia in the USSR. The Dilemma of Dominance* (New York: Pergamon).

Andreyuk, G. P. (1966), 'Vydvizhenchestvo i ego rol' v formirovanii intelligentsii (1921–32gg.)', *Iz istorii sovetskoy intelligentsii* (Moscow).

Arendt, H. (1958), *The Origins of Totalitarianism* (Cleveland, Ohio: World Publishing Company).

Armstrong, J. A. (1959), *The Soviet Bureaucratic Élite: A Case Study of the Ukrainian Apparatus* (New York: Praeger).

Aron, R. (1950), 'Social structure and ruling class', *British Journal of Sociology*, vol. 1, no. 1 (pt 1), vol. 1, no. 2 (pt 2).

Arutyunyan, Yu. V. (1969), 'Konkretno-sotsiologicheskoe issledovanie natsional'nykh otnosheniy', *Voprosy filosofii*, no. 12.

Arutyunyan, Yu. V. (1971), *Sotsial'naya struktura sel'skogo naseleniya* (Moscow).

Arutyunyan, Yu. V. (1974), 'O razvitii i sblizhenie kul'tury Sovetskikh natsii', *Sotsiologicheskie issledovaniya*, no. 2.

Aspaturian, V. V. (1968), 'The non-Russian nationalities', in A. Kassof (ed.), *Prospects for Soviet Society* (London: Pall Mall Press).

Bahro, R. (1978), *The Alternative in Eastern Europe* (London: New Left Books).

Bain, G. S. (1970), *The Growth of White-Collar Unionism* (London: Oxford University Press).

Bain, G. S., Bacon, R. and Pimlott, J. (1972), 'The labour force', in A. H. Halsey (ed.), *Trends in British Society since 1900* (London: Macmillan).

Barber, B. (1957), *Social Stratification* (New York: Harcourt, Brace & World).

Baykov, A. (1947), *The Development of the Soviet Economic System: An Essay on the Experience of Planning in the USSR* (Cambridge: Cambridge University Press).

Bellis, P. (1979), *Marxism and the USSR* (London: Macmillan).

Bendix, R. and Lipset, S. M. (1959), *Social Mobility in Industrial Society* (Berkeley, Calif.: University of California Press).

Bergson, A. (1944), *The Structure of Soviet Wages, A Study in Socialist Economics* (Cambridge, Mass.: Harvard University Press).

Béteille, A. (ed.) (1969), *Social Inequality* (Harmondsworth: Penguin).

Bialer, S. (1966), 'Soviet political élite: concept, sample, case study' (PhD dissertation, Columbia University).

Bialer, S. (1980a), 'Comment – the impact of common RSFSR/USSR institutions', in Allworth, op. cit., 1980.

Bialer, S. (1980b), *Stalin's Successors: Leadership Stability and Change in the Soviet Union* (Cambridge: Cambridge University Press).

Bienstock, G., Schwarz, S. M. and Yugow, A. (1948), *Management in Russian Industry and Agriculture* (Ithaca, NY: Cornell University Press).

Bilinsky, J. (1967), 'The rulers and the ruled', *Problems of Communism*, vol. 16, no. 5.

Binns, P. and Haynes, M. (1980), 'New theories of Eastern European class societies', *International Socialism*, series 2, no. 7.

Blumberg, P. (1968), *Industrial Democracy: The Sociology of Participation* (London: Constable).

Bolgov, A. V. (1962), 'Preodolenie sushchestvennykh razlichiy mezhdu gorodom i derevney', *Ot sotsializma k kommunizmu* (Moscow).

Bottomore, T. B. (1965), *Classes in Modern Society* (London: Allen & Unwin).

Brudny, V. I. and Kaganov, A. B. (1977), 'Sotsial'nye istochniki formirovaniya studenchestva', *Sotsiologicheskie issledovaniya, no. 2*.

Brzezinski, Z. and Huntington, S. P. (1964), *Political Power: USA/USSR* (London: Chatto & Windus).

Bubnov, A. (1930), 'VKP(B)', *Bol'shaya Sovetskaya Entsiklopediya*, Vol. 11 (Moscow).

Burnham, J. (1941), *The Managerial Revolution* (Bloomington, Ind.: Indiana University Press; Harmondsworth: Penguin, 1945).

Carlo, A. (1974), 'The socio-economic nature of the USSR', *Telos*, no. 21.

Carr, E. H. (1950), *The Bolshevik Revolution 1917–23*, Vol. 1 (London: Macmillan, Harmondsworth: Penguin, 1966).

Central Statistical Office (1980), *Annual Abstract of Statistics* (London: HMSO).

Chapman, J. G. (1970), *Wage Variation in Soviet Industry: The Impact of the 1956–1960 Wage Reform* (Santa Monica, Calif.: Rand Corporation).

Chapman, J. G. (1979), 'Recent trends in the Soviet industrial wage structure', in Kahan and Ruble, op. cit., 1979.

Charlton, K. (1968), 'Polytechnic education', *International Review of Education*, vol. 14, no. 1.

Churchward, L. G. (1968), 'Bureaucracy – USA: USSR', *Co-existence*, vol. 5, no. 2.

Clem, R. S. (1980), 'Economic development of the Russian homeland: regional growth in the Soviet Union', in Allworth, op. cit., 1980.

Cliff, T. (1964), *Russia: A Marxist Analysis* (London: Socialist Review Publishers).

Cohn-Bendit, G. and D. (1969), *Obsolete Communism: The Left-Wing Alternative* (Harmondsworth: Penguin).

Connor, W. D. (1979), *Socialism, Politics and Equality. Hierarchy and Change in Eastern Europe and the USSR* (New York: Columbia University Press).

Conquest, R. (1967), *Soviet Nationalities Policy in Practice* (London: Bodley Head).

Crosland, C. A. R. (1956), *The Future of Socialism* (London: Cape).

Dahrendorf, R. (1969), 'On the origin of inequality among men', in Béteille, op. cit., 1969.

Deputaty verkhovnogo soveta SSSR (1966 and 1979) (Moscow).

Dewar, M. (1962), 'Labour and wage reforms in the USSR', *Studies in the Soviet Union* (Munich), vol. 3, no. 3.

De Witt, N. (1961), *Educational and Professional Manpower in the USSR* (Washington: National Research Council).

Djilas, M. (1966), *The New Class, an Analysis of the Communist System* (London: Allen & Unwin).

Dodge, N. T. (1966), *Women in the Soviet Economy* (Baltimore, Md: Johns Hopkins University Press).

Drobizhev, V. Z. (1961), 'Rol' rabochego klassa SSSR v formirovanii komandnykh kadrov sotsialisticheskoy promyshlennosti (1917–1936)', *Istoriya SSSR*, no. 4.

Dukhovoe razvitie lichnosti (1967) (Sverdlovsk).

Ellman, M. (1980), 'A note on the distribution of earnings in the USSR under Brezhnev', *Slavic Review*, vol. 39, no. 4.

Elmeev, V. Ya., *et al.* (1965), *Kommunizm i preodolenie razdeleniya mezhdu umstvennym i fizicheskim trudom* (Leningrad).

Engels, F. (1951), 'The origin of the family, private property and the state', in Marx and Engels, *Selected Works*, Vol. 2 (Moscow: Foreign Languages Publishing House).

Evans, B. A., Jr (1977), 'Developed socialism in Soviet ideology', *Soviet Studies*, vol. 29, no. 3.

Farrell, R. B. (1970), *Political Leadership in Eastern Europe and the Soviet Union* (London: Butterworth).

Feldmesser, R. A. (1957), 'Social status and access to higher education', *Harvard Educational Review*, vol. 27, no. 2.

Feldmesser, R. A. (1966), 'Towards the classless society?', in R. Bendix and S. M. Lipset (eds), *Class, Status and Power* (London: Routledge & Kegan Paul).

Ferge, S. (1966), *Valosag* (Budapest).

Feshbach, M. and Rapawy, S. (1976), 'Soviet population and manpower trends and policies', in Joint Economic Committee, US Congress, *Soviet Economy in New Perspective* (Washington, DC: Government Printing Office).

Filippov, F. R. (1977), 'Rol' vysshey shkoly v izmenenii sotsial'noy struktury sovetskogo obschestva (itogi vsesoyuznogo issledovaniya'), *Sotsiologicheskie issledovaniya*, no. 2.

Filippov, F. R. (1980), 'Formirovanie popolneniy sotsialisticheskoy intelligentsii', *Sotsiologicheskie issledovaniya*, no. 2.

Fisher, A. W. (1979), 'The Crimean Tatars, the USSR and Turkey', in McCagg and Silver, op. cit., 1979.

Fleron, F. J. (1970), 'Representation of career-types in Soviet political leadership', in Farrell, R. B. (ed.), *Political Leadership in Eastern Europe and the Soviet Union* (London: Butterworth).

Fogarty, M. P., Rapoport, R. and Rapoport, R. N. (1971), *Sex, Career and Family* (London: Allen & Unwin).

Friedgut, T. H. (1979), *Political Participation in the USSR* (Princeton, NJ.: Princeton University Press).

Friedrich, C. J. (1972), 'In defence of a concept', in L. Schapiro (ed.), *Political Opposition in One Party States* (London: Macmillan).

Friedrich, C. J. and Brzezinski, Z. K. (1966), *Totalitarian Dictatorship and Autocracy* (New York: Praeger).

Friedrich, C. J., Curtis, M. and Barber, B. R. (1969), *Totalitarianism in Perspective: Three Views* (New York: Praeger).

Gehlen, M. P. (1969), *The Communist Party of the Soviet Union* (Bloomington, Ind.: Indiana University Press).

Gellner, E. (ed.) (1980), *Soviet and Western Anthropology* (London: Duckworth).

Gentvaynite, V., Matulenis, A., Tal'yunayte (1977), 'Sotsial'naya orientatsiya vypushikov srednikh shkol', *Sotsiologicheskie issledovaniya*, no.2.

George, V. and Manning, N. (1980), *Socialism, Social Welfare and the Soviet Union* (London: Routledge & Kegan Paul).

Gerschenkron, A. (1947), 'The rate of industrial growth in Russia since 1885', *Journal of Economic History*, vol. 7 (supplement).

Giddens, A. (1973), *The Class Structure of the Advanced Societies* (London: Hutchinson).

Glezerman, G. (1968), 'Sotsial'naya struktura sotsialisticheskogo obshchestva', *Kommunist*, no. 13. Also in *Soviet News* (London), 12 November 1968.

Glowacki, W. (1959), 'Pracownicy "Kasprzaka" o zarobkach', in *Zycie Gospodarcze*, no. 14 (5 April).

Goldthorpe, J. H. (1967), 'Social stratification in industrial society', in R. Bendix and S. M. Lipset (eds), *Class, Status and Power: Social Stratification in Comparative Perspective* (London: Routledge & Kegan Paul).

Goldthorpe, J. H. *et al.* (1969), *The Affluent Worker in the Class Structure*, Vol. 3 (Cambridge: Cambridge University Press).

Gordon, L. A. and Klopov, E. V. (1973), 'Some problems of the social structure of the Soviet working class', in Yanowitch, M. and Fisher, W. (eds), *Social Stratification and Mobility in the USSR* (New York: International Arts and Sciences Press).

Gouldner, A. W. (1979), *The Future of Intellectuals and the Rise of the New Class* (London: Macmillan).

Gransow, V. (1980), 'Political culture in the GDR. Propositions for empirical research'. Paper presented at Second World Congress for Soviet and East European Studies, Garmisch-Partenkirchen.

Gruzdeva, E. B. (1975), 'Osobennosti obraza zhizni "intelligentnykh rabochikh"', *Robochi klass i sovremenny mir*, no. 2 (26).

Guryanov, S. T. (1966), 'Vertical mobility of employees in an enterprise', in G. V. Osipov (ed.), *Industry and Labour in the USSR* (London: Tavistock).

Harasymiw, B. (1969), '*Nomenklatura*: the Soviet Party's leadership recruitment system', *Canadian Journal of Political Science*, vol. 2, no. 3.

Harasymiw, B. (1980), 'Have women's chances for political recruitment in the USSR really improved?', in Yedlin, op. cit., 1980.

Heath, A. (1981), *Social Mobility* (London: Fontana).

Hill, I. H. (1975), 'The end of the Russian peasantry?', *Soviet Studies*, vol. 27, no. 1.

Hirszowicz, M. (1980), *The Bureaucratic Leviathan: A Study in the Sociology of Communism* (Oxford: Martin Robertson).

Hobsbawm, E. J. (1968), *Industry and Empire* (London: Weidenfeld & Nicolson; Harmondsworth: Penguin, 1969).

Hough, J. F. (1969), *The Soviet Prefects: The Local Party Organs in Industrial*

Decision-Making (Cambridge, Mass.: Harvard University Press).

Hough, J. F. (1976), 'Political participation in the Soviet Union', *Soviet Studies*, vol. 28, no. 1.

Hough, J. F. (1977), *The Soviet Union and Social Science Theory* (Cambridge, Mass.: Harvard University Press).

Hough, J. F. (1979), 'The generation gap and the Brezhnev succession', *Problems of Communism*, vol. 28, no. 1.

Hungarian Central Statistical Office (1967), *Social Stratification in Hungary* (Budapest).

Inkeles, A. and Rossi, P. H. (1956), 'National comparisons of occupational prestige', *American Journal of Sociology*, vol. 61, no. 4.

'International study of opinion makers (Yugoslav section)' (1969). Sponsored by Columbia University (duplicated paper, London School of Economics and Political Science).

Iovchuk, M. T., Kogan, L. and Rutkevich, M. N. (1962), 'Pod'em kul' turnotekhnicheskogo urovnya rabochego klassa i ego rol' v soedinenii fizicheskogo i umstvennogo truda v SSSR', *Ot sotsializma k kommunizmu* (Moscow).

Jancar, B. W. (1978), *Women under Communism* (Baltimore, Md: Johns Hopkins University Press).

Jenkins, R. (1952), 'Equality', *New Fabian Essays* (London: Fabian Society).

Kahan, A. and Ruble, B. A. (1979), *Industrial Labor in the USSR* (New York: Pergamon).

Karapetyan, S. A. (1968), 'Modelirovanie semeynykh dokhodov po materialam perepisi naseleniya' (Candidate's dissertation, Rostov on Don University).

Karcz, J. F. (1966), 'Seven years on the farm: retrospective and prospects', in Joint Economic Committee, US Congress, *New Directions in the Soviet Economy* (Washington, DC: Government Printing Office).

Katuntseva, N. M. (1966), *Rol' rabochikh fakul'tetov v formirovanie kadrov narodnoy intelligentsii v SSSR* (Moscow).

Kemeny, I. (1979), 'Poverty in Hungary', *Social Science Information*, vol. 18, no. 2.

Kharchev, A. G. (1965), 'O putyakh dal'neyshego ukrepleniya sem'i v SSSR', *Sotsial'nye issledovaniya*, no. 1.

Klassy, sotsial'nye sloi i gruppy v SSSR (1968), Moscow.

Kogan, L. N. (1977), 'Sblizhenie sotsial'nykh grupp v sfere sotsialisticheskoy kul'tury', *Sotsiologicheskie issledovaniya*, no. 2.

Kolankiewicz, G. (1979), 'Socialist equality: changing prospects for egalitarianism in contemporary Polish society'. Paper presented to American Association for the Advancement of Slavic Studies, New Haven, Conn.

Kolankiewicz, G. (1980), 'The bureaucratisation of political participation in Poland'. Paper presented at Second World Congress for Soviet and East European Studies, Garmisch-Partenkirchen.

Konrad, G. and Szelenyi, I. (1979), *The Intellectuals on the Road to Class Power* (Brighton, Sussex: Harvester).

Kornhauser, W. (1960), *The Politics of Mass Society* (London: Routledge & Kegan Paul).

Kory, W. B. (1980), 'Spatial diffusion of Russians in the USSR', in Allworth, op. cit., 1980.

Kostin, L. (1960), *Wages in the Soviet Union* (Moscow).

'KPSS v tsifrakh (1961–1964 gody)' (1965), *Partiynaya zhizn'*, no. 10.

KPSS (1966), *XXIII S'ezd*, Vols 1 and 2 (Moscow).

KPSS (1969), *Naglyadnoe posobie partiynomu stroitel'stvu* (Moscow).

Kropotkin, Peter (1888), *The Wage System* (London: Freedom Press).

Kuron, J. and Modzelewski, K. (1968), *An Open Letter to the Party* (London: International Socialism Publication).

Lane, C. (1978), *Christian Religion in The Soviet Union* (London: Allen & Unwin).

Lane, D. (1969), *The Roots of Russian Communism* (Assen: Van Gorcum).

Lane, D. (1973), 'The impact of revolution: the case of selection of students for higher education in Soviet Russia, 1917–1928', *Sociology*, vol. 7, no. 2.

Lane, D. (1976), *The Socialist Industrial State: Towards a Political Sociology of State Socialism* (London: Allen & Unwin).

Lane, D. (1978), *Politics and Society in the USSR* (London: Martin Robertson).

Lane, D. (1981), *Leninism: A Sociological Interpretation* (Cambridge: Cambridge University Press).

Lane, D. and O'Dell, F. (1978), *The Soviet Industrial Worker* (London: Martin Robertson).

Lapidus, G. W. (1978), *Women in Soviet Society* (Berkeley, Calif.: University of California Press).

Lapidus, G. W. (1980), 'Sex difference in the economic returns of education in the USSR'. Paper presented at Second World Congress for Soviet and East European Studies, Garmisch-Partenkirchen.

Lenin, V. I. (1965), 'Economics and politics in the era of the dictatorship of the proletariat', *Collected Works*, Vol. 30 (Moscow).

Lenski, G. E. (1966), *Power and Privilege, A Theory of Social Stratification* (New York: McGraw-Hill).

Lewis, P. (1973), 'The peasantry', in D. Lane and G. Kolankiewicz (eds), *Social Groups in Polish Society* (London: Macmillan).

Lewis, R. A. (1980), 'Comment – intensifying Russian ethnic identity by dispersion', in Allworth, op. cit., 1980.

Libaridian, G. J. (1979), 'Armenia and Armenians: a divided homeland and a dispersed nation', in McCagg and Silver, op. cit., 1979.

Lipset, S. M. (1969), *Revolution and Counter-Revolution* (London: Heinemann).

Lipset, S. M. and Dobson, R. B. (1973), 'Social stratification and sociology in the Soviet Union', *Survey*, vol. 19 (Summer).

Lobodzinska, B. (1970), 'Trends in the homogeneity and equality in urban marriages in Poland'. Paper presented at World Congress of Sociology, Varna.

Lockwood, D. (1958), *The Blackcoated Worker* (London: Allen & Unwin).

Lukina, V. I. (1979), 'Kolichestvo detey v sem'e i sotsial'no – professional'nye peremeshcheniya roditeley', *Sotsiologicheskie issledovaniya*, no. 4.

McAuley, A. (1977), 'The distribution of earnings and incomes in the Soviet Union', *Soviet Studies*, vol. 29, no. 2.

McAuley, A. (1979), *Economic Welfare in the Soviet Union* (London: Allen & Unwin).

McAuley, A. (1981), *Women's Work and Wages in the Soviet Union* (London: Allen & Unwin).

McCagg, W. O., Jr and Silver, B. D. (1979), *Soviet Asian Ethnic Frontiers* (New York: Pergamon).

Machonin, P. (1969), 'The social structure of contemporary Czechoslovak society', *Czechoslovak Economic Papers*, no. 11.

Machonin, P. (1970), 'Social stratification in contemporary Czechoslovakia', *American Journal of Sociology*, vol. 75, no. 5.

Maher, J. E. (1980), 'The social composition of women deputies in Soviet elective politics', in Yedlin, op. cit., 1980.

Mandel, E. (1969), *The Inconsistencies of State Capitalism* (London: International Marxist Group).

Mandel, E. (1979–80), 'Once again on the Trotskyist definition of the social nature of the Soviet Union', *Critique*, no. 12.

Manevich, E. L. (1966), *Problemy obshchestvennogo truda v SSSR* (Moscow).

Marksistsko-leninskaya filosofiya i sotsiologiya v SSSR i Evropeiskikh sotsialisticheskikh stran (1965) (Moscow).

Marx, K. (1958*a*), 'The eighteenth Brumaire of Louis Napoleon', in Marx and Engels, *Selected Works*, Vol. 1 (Moscow: Foreign Languages Publishing House).

Marx, K. (1958*b*), 'Preface to *A Contribution to the Critique of Political Economy*', in Marx and Engels, *Selected Works*, Vol. 1 (Moscow: Foreign Languages Publishing House).

Marx, K. (1867, repr. 1962), *Capital*, Vol. 3 (Moscow: Foreign Languages Publishing House).

Marx, K. and Engels, F. (1965), *The German Ideology* (London: Lawrence & Wishart).

Matthews, M. (1978), *Privilege in the Soviet Union* (London: Allen & Unwin).

Medvedev, R. (1971), *Let History Judge* (New York: Knopf).

Meikle, S. (1981), 'Has Marxism a future?', *Critique*, no. 13.

Meissner, B. (1966), 'Totalitarian rule and social change', *Problems of Communism*, vol. 15, no. 6.

Melotti, U. (1977), *Marx and the Third World* (London: Macmillan).

Melotti, U. (1980), 'Socialism and bureaucratic collectivism in the Third World', *Telos*, no. 43.

Meyer, A. G. (1964), 'USSR incorporated', in D. W. Treadgold (ed.), *The Development of the USSR, an Exchange of Views* (Seattle, Wash.: University of Washington Press).

Milic, V. (1965–6), 'General trends in social mobility in Yugoslavia', *Acta Sociologica*, vol. 9.

Miller, S. M. (1960), 'Comparative social mobility', *Current Sociology*, vol. 9, no. 1.

Mil'tykbaev, Kh. M. (1965), *Izmenenie sotsial'noy struktury obshchestva v period razvernutogo kommunisticheskogo stroitel'stva* (Tashkent).

Molyneaux, M. (n.d.), 'Women's emancipation under socialism: a model for the

Third World?' (University of Essex, Department of Sociology, unpublished paper).

Müller, V. (1969), 'The price of egalitarianism', *Problems of Communism*, vol. 18, nos 4–5.

Musatov, I. M. (1967), *Sotsial'nye problemy trudovykh resursov v SSSR* (Moscow).

Narodnoe obrazovanie, nauka i kul'tura v SSSR (1977) (Moscow).

Naselenie SSSR po dannym vsesoyuznoy perepisi naseleniya 1979g (1980) (abbreviated as *Naselenie*) (Moscow).

NATO (1979), *Regional Development in the USSR. Trends and Prospects* (Newtonville, Mass.: Oriental Research Partners).

Nove, A. and Newth, J. A. (1967), *The Soviet Middle East, A Model for Development* (London: Allen & Unwin).

Oakley, A. (1981), *Subject Women* (Oxford: Martin Robertson).

Osipov, G. V. and Frolov, S. F. (1966), 'Vnerabochee vremya i ego ispol'zovania', in *Sotsiologiya v SSSR*, Vol. 2 (Moscow).

Ossowski, S. (1963), *Class Structure in the Social Consciousness* (London: Routledge & Kegan Paul).

Pankratova, M. G. and Yankova, Z. A. (1978), 'Sovetskaya zhenshchina', *Sotsiologicheskie issledovaniya*, no. 1.

Parkin, F. (1969), 'Class stratification in socialist societies', *British Journal of Sociology*, vol. 20, no. 4.

Parkin, F. (1971), *Class Inequality and Political Order, Social Stratification in Capitalist and Communist Societies* (London: Macgibbon & Kee).

Parkin, F. (1979), *Marxism and Class Theory: A Bourgeois Critique* (London: Tavistock).

Parsons, T. (1954), 'An analytical approach to the theory of social stratification', in *Essays in Sociological Theory*, rev. edn (Glencoe, Ill.: The Free Press).

Pod'yachich, P. G. (1961), *Naselenie SSSR* (Moscow).

Popova, I. M. and Moin, V. B. (1979), 'Prestizh i privlekatel'nost' professiy', *Sotsiologicheskie issledovaniya*, no. 4.

Porket, J. L. (1981), 'Old age pensions in the USSR and Eastern Europe'. Paper presented at Annual Conference of British Sociological Association.

Problemy izmeneniya sotsial'noy struktury Sovetskogo obshchestva, (1968) (Moscow).

Programme of the Communist Party of the Soviet Union, The (1961) (London: Soviet Booklet, no. 83).

Protsessy izmeneniya sotsial'noy struktury v Sovetskom obshchestve (1967) Sverdlovsk).

Radio Liberty Research (1980), 'Sakharov and the non-Russian peoples of the USSR', Radio Liberty Research 41/80 (Munich).

Rahr, A. G. and Scarlis, S. (1981), *A Biographic Directory of One Hundred Leading Soviet Officials* (Munich: Radio Liberty Research Bulletin).

Rakowska-Harmstone, T. (1974), 'The dialectics of nationalism in the USSR', *Problems of Communism*, vol. 23, no. 3.

Rashin, A. G. (1961), 'Dinamika promyshlennykh kadrov SSSR za 1917–1958 gg', *Izmeneniya v chislennosti i sostave Sovetskogo rabochego klassa* (Moscow).

Rasiak, R. O. (1980), '"The Soviet people": multiethnic alternative or ruse?', in Allworth, op. cit., 1980.

Riddell, D. (1968), 'Social self-government: the background of theory and practice in Yugoslav socialism', *British Journal of Sociology*, vol. 19, no. 1.

Rigby, T. H. (1968), *Communist Party Membership in the USSR: 1917-67* (Princeton, NJ: Princeton University Press).

Rigby, T. H. (1972), '"Totalitarianism" and change in communist systems', *Comparative Politics* (April).

Rizzi, B. (1939), *La Bureaucratisation du monde* (Paris).

Rogachev, P. M. and Sverdlin, M. A. (1966), 'O ponyatii "Natsiya"', *Voprosy istorii*, no. 1.

Rossi, P. H. and Inkeles, A. (1957), 'Multidimensional ratings of occupations', *Sociometry*, vol. 20, no. 3.

Rywkin, M. (1979), 'Central Asia and Soviet manpower', *Problems of Communism*, vol. 28, no. 1.

Rywkin, M. (1980), 'The Russian-wide Soviet Federated Socialist Republic (RSFSR): privileged or underprivileged?' in Allworth, op. cit., 1980.

Sadowski, M. (1968), 'Przemiany spoleczne a partie politiczne PRL', *Studia Sociologiczne*, no. 30-1.

Safar, Z. et al. (1970), 'Basic data on social differentiation in the Czechoslovak socialist society'. Paper presented at World Congress of Sociology, Varna.

Safar, Z. (1971), 'Different approaches to the measurement of social differentiation and social mobility in the Czech Slovak socialist society', *Quality and Quantity*, vol. 5.

Saifulin, M. (ed.) (1967), *The Soviet Parliament* (Moscow: Progress Publishers).

Sarapata, A. (1966), 'Stratification and social mobility', in Jan Szczepanksi (ed.), *Empirical Sociology in Poland* (Warsaw: Polish Scientific Publishers).

Schachtman, M. (1962), *The Bureaucratic Revolution* (New York: Donald Press).

Schapiro, L. (1960), *The Communist Party of the Soviet Union* (London: Constable).

Schlesinger, R. (1956), *The Nationalities Problem and Soviet Administration* (London: Routledge & Kegan Paul).

Schnabl, S. (1978), *Man and Frau intim* (Berlin).

Schneller, G. K. (1966), 'The Politburo', in H. D. Lasswell and D. Lerner (eds), *World Revolutionary Élites, Studies in Coercive Ideological Movements* (Cambridge, Mass.: MIT).

Schroeder, G. (1979), 'Regional differences in incomes in the USSR in the 1970s', in NATO, op. cit., 1979.

Semenov, V. S. (1962), 'Preobrazovaniya v rabochem klasse i intelligentsii v protsesse perekhoda k kommunizmu', *Ot sotsializma k kommunizmu* (Moscow).

Semenov, V. S. (1964), 'O partii i intelligentsii v Sovetskom Soyuze', *Marksistskaya i burzhuaznaya sotsiologiya segodnya* (Moscow).

Semenov, V. S. (1968), 'Rabochi klass-vedushchaya sila Sovetskogo obshchestva', *Klassy, sotsial'nye sloi i gruppy v SSSR* (Moscow).

Sheremet, I. I. (1977), 'Sotsial'ny sostav studenchestva', *Sotsiologicheskie issledovaniya*, no. 2.

Shkaratan, O. I. (1967), 'Sotsial'naya struktura Sovetskogo rabochego klassa', *Voprosy filosofii*, no. 1.

Shkaratan, O. I. (1970), *Problemy sotsial'noy struktury rabochego klassa SSSR* (Moscow).

Shkaratan, O. I. (1973), 'Sources of social differentiation of the working class in Soviet society', reprinted in M. Yanowitch and W. A. Fisher (eds), *Social Stratification and Mobility in the USSR* (New York: International Arts and Sciences Press).

Shkaratan, O. I., Filippova, O. V. and Demidova, L. G. (1980), 'Sotsial'ny sloy i professiya', *Sotsiologicheskie issledovaniya*, no. 3.

Shkaratan, O. I. and Rukavishnikov, V. O. (1977), 'Sotsial'nye sloi v klassovoy strukture sotsialisticheskogo obshchestva', *Sotsiologicheskie issledovaniya*, no. 2.

Shmelev, G. (1965), 'Ekonomicheskaya rol' lichnogo podsobnogo khozyaystva', *Voprosy ekonomiki*, no. 4.

Shtraks, G. M. (1966), *Sotsial'noe edinstvo i protivorechiya sotsialisticheskogo obshchestva* (Moscow).

Shubkin, V. N. (1965), 'Molodezh' vstupaet v zhizn'', *Voprosy filosofii*, no. 5.

Shubkin, V. N. (1966), 'Social mobility and choice of occupation', in G. V. Osipov (ed.), *Industry and Labour in the USSR* (London: Tavistock).

Sik, O. (1967), *Plan and Market under Socialism* (New York: International Arts and Sciences Press).

Simush, P. I. (1976), *Sotsial'ny portret sovetskogo krest'yanstva* (Moscow).

Skilling, H. G. (1966), *The Governments of Communist East Europe* (New York: Crowell).

Skilling, H. G. and Griffiths, F. (1971), *Interest Groups in Soviet Politics* (Princeton, NJ: Princeton University Press).

Slomczynski, K. (1970), 'Socio-occupational differentiation and education, authority, income and prestige'. Paper presented at World Congress of Sociology, Varna.

Slomczynski, K. and W. Wesolowski (1974), *Reduction of Inequalities and Status Inconsistency* (Toronto: International Sociological Association).

Smirnov, G. (1965), 'Dinamika rosta rabochego klassa i izmenenie ego professional'nogo-kvalifikatsionnogo sostava', in *Sotsiologiya v SSSR*, Vol. 1 (Moscow).

Stalin, I. V. (1952), *Economic Problems of Socialism* (Moscow: Foreign Languages Publishing House).

Stalin, I. V. (1955), 'Talk with Emil Ludwig', *Collected Works*, Vol. 13 (Moscow: Foreign Languages Publishing House).

Stalin, I. V. (1967), 'O proekte konstitutsii Soyuza SSSR', *Sochineniya*, vol. 1, no. 24 (Stanford University Press for the Hoover Institute, Stanford, Calif.).

Staniszkis, J. (1979), 'Adaptational superstructure – the problem of negative self-regulation', in J. J. Wiatr (ed.), *Polish Essays in the Methodology of the Social Sciences* (Dordrecht: Reidel).

Staniszkis, J. (1981), 'The evolution of working-class protest in Poland: sociological reflections on the Gdansk–Szczecin case, August 1980', *Soviet Studies*, vol. 33, no. 2.

Staroverov, V. I. (1977), 'Tendentsii izmeneniya sotsial'noy struktury sel'skogo naseleniya SSSR na etape razvitogo sotsializma', *Sotsiologicheskie issledovaniya*, no. 2.

Staroverov, V. I. (1978), *Sotsial'naya struktura sel'skogo naseleniya SSSR na etape razvitogo sotsializma* (Moscow).

Stewart, P. D. (1968), *Political Power in the Soviet Union (Indianapolis, Ind.;* New York: Bobbs-Merrill).

Struktura Sovetskoy intelligentsii (1970) (Minsk).

Sukharevski, B. M. (1968), 'Zarabotnaya plata i material'naya zainterovannost'', *Trud i zarabotnaya plata v SSSR* (Moscow).

Swafford, M. (1978), 'Sex differences in Soviet earnings', *American Sociological Review*, vol. 43.

Szczepanski, J. (1970), *Polish Society* (New York: Random House).

Szesztay, A. (1967), *Veszprèmben végertek* (Budapest).

Tashtemirov, U. (1981), 'Motivy razvodov v odnonatsional'nykh uzbekskikh sem'yakh', *Sotsiologicheskie issledovaniya*, no. 2.

Teague, L. (1981), 'The Central Committee and Central Auditing Commission elected at the Twenty-Sixth Congress of the CPSU', Radio Liberty Research 171/81 (Munich).

Ticktin, H. (1973), 'Towards a political economy of the USSR', *Critique*, no. 1.

Ticktin, H. (1981), 'The victory and the tragedy of the Polish working class', *Critique*, no. 13.

Tkach, Ya. M. (1967), 'Roditeli o sud'bakh svoikh detey', *Protsessy izmeneniya sotsial'noy struktury v sovetskom obshchestve* (Sverdlovsk).

Trotsky, L. (1945), *The Revolution Betrayed: The Soviet Union, What It Is and Where It Is Going* (London: Pioneer).

Trud v SSSR (1968) (Moscow).

Trufanov, I. P. (1973), *Problemy byta gorodskogo naseleniya SSSR* (Leningrad).

Tsentral'noe statisticheskoe upravlenie (1962) (abbreviated to Tsentral'noe), *Itogi vsesoyuznoy perepisi naseleniya 1959g. SSSR (svodny tom)* (Moscow).

Tsentral'noe (1963), *Narodnoe khozyaystvo SSSR v 1962g* (Moscow).

Tsentral'noe (1966), *Narodnoe khozyaystvo SSSR v 1965g* (Moscow).

Tsentral'noe (1967), *Strana Sovetov za 50 let: sbornik statisticheskikh materialov* (Moscow).

Tsentral'noe (1972), *Itogi vsesoyuznoy perepisi naseleniya 1970g*, Tom 3 (Vol. 3).

Tsentral'noe (1973), Tom 6 (Vol. 6), Tom 4 (Vol. 4), Tom 7 (Vol. 7).

Tsentral'noe (1979), *Narodnoe khozyaystvo SSSR v 1978g* (Moscow).

Tsentral'noe (1980), *Narodnoe khozyaystvo SSSR v 1979g* (Moscow).

Tumin, M. M. (1964), 'Ethnic groups', in J. Gould and W. L. Kolb (eds), *A Dictionary of the Social Sciences* (London: Tavistock).

United Nations (1967), *Economic Survey of Europe in 1965* (Geneva: UN).

Vodzinskaya, V. V. (1973), 'Orientations to occupations', in M. Yanowitch and W. A. Fisher (eds), *Social Stratification and Mobility in the USSR* (New York: International Arts and Sciences Press).

Vol'fson, S. Ya. (1937), *Sem'ya i Brak* (Moscow).

Voritsyn, S. (1969), 'The present composition of the Party Central Committee: a brief sociological analysis', *Bulletin of the Institute for the Study of the USSR*, vol. 26.

Vorontsov, A. V. (1980), 'Razvitie dukhovnykh potrebnostey kolkhoznogo krest'yanstvo nechernozemnoy zony RSFSR', *Sotsiologicheskie issledovaniya*, no. 3.

Wesolowski, W. (1966), 'Changes in the class structure in Poland', in J. Szczepanksi (ed.), *Empirical Sociology in Poland* (Warsaw: Polish Scientific Publications).

Wesolowski, W. (1969), 'The notions of strata and class in socialist society', in Béteille, op. cit., 1969.

Wesolowski, W. (1979), *Classes, Strata and Power*, trans. and with an intro. by G. Kolankiewicz (London: Routledge & Kegan Paul).

Wesolowski, W. and Slomczynski, K. M. (1977), *Investigations on Class Structure and Social Stratification in Poland 1945–75* (Warsaw).

Wheeler, G. (1964), *The Modern History of Soviet Central Asia* (London: Weidenfeld & Nicolson).

White, G. (1978), 'Politics and social status in China', *Pacific Affairs*, vol. 51, no. 4.

Widerszpil, S. *et al.* (1959), *Zycie Gospodarcze*, no. 25.

Wilber, Charles K. (1969), *The Soviet Model and Undeveloped Countries* (Chapel Hill, NC: University of North Carolina Press).

Wiles, P. J. D. and Markowski, S. (1971), 'Income distribution under communism and capitalism; some facts about Poland, the UK, the USA and the USSR', *Soviet Studies*, vol. 22, no. 3.

Woodcock, G. (1962), *Anarchism* (Cleveland, Ohio: World Publishing Co.; Harmondsworth: Penguin, 1963).

Wright, E. O. (1976), 'Class boundaries in advanced capitalist societies', *New Left Review*, no. 98.

Yanowitch, M. (1977), *Social and Economic Inequality in the Soviet Union* (London: Martin Robertson).

Yedlin, T. (1980), *Women in Eastern Europe and the Soviet Union* (New York: Praeger).

Zagorski, K. (1970), *Social Mobility and Changes in the Structure of Planning Society* (Warsaw).

Zagorski, K. (1974), *Changes of the Socio-Occupational Mobility in Poland* (Jablonna: GUS [Central Statistical Office]).

Zhenshchiny i deti v SSSR (1969) (Moscow).

'Zhenshchiny v SSSR' (1965), *Vestnik statistiki*, no. 2.

Zhenshchiny v SSSR (1975) (Moscow).

'Zhenshchiny v SSSR' (1981), *Vestnik statistiki*, no. 1.

Zukin, S. (1978), 'Problems of social class under socialism', *Theory and Society*, no. 3.

Index

and Soviet theory 133–4, 135, 152–3
see also property

Parkin, F. 140–1, 142, 144
participation
and decision-making 51–2, 145–6
peasantry 37–8
and Russian Revolution 13–4
and Soviet social structure 26, 38–45
people's democracy *see* state-socialist societies
Poland
class perceptions 100
collectivism 46
inter-marriage and social groups 97–9
occupational prestige 68, 70–1
participation and decision-making 145–6
political party composition 117–8
political tensions 135, 138–9, 151
social mobility studies 105–6, 107–8
socialism in 28, 31–2
wage differentials 60–1, 101–2
Polish United Workers Party 117–8
Politburo
educational profiles 120
ethnic composition of Praesidium 92–3
social composition of 119–20, 121
political consciousness
and occupation 118
and women 80
in urban and rural populations 44–5
population
composition in USSR 82–3
distribution in Soviet Russia 42
social structure in Soviet Russia 15
poverty
in Hungary 60
in Russia 59–60
prestige
and occupation 66–70
production
and 'bureaucratic collectivism' 131
and class 4
and 'party elite' 135
Asiatic method of 130, 134
proletariat 7
dictatorship of 10–24, 25
education of 18–9
English 65
'proletarian internationalism' 84–5
property

and socialist theory 152–3
'Red Directors' 16
revolution
and need for education 16, 18–9
Russian 9, 10–3
Rizzi, B. 126
'State-capitalist' theory of socialism 129, 134–6
Russia
and Marxist theory 6–33
Civil War 12
economic development 6–7, 105
industrialisation 14–5
proletariat 7
social mobility 19–20
social revolution 10–3, 23
wages 20–2
see also Union of Soviet Socialist Republics
Russian Communist Party *see* Bolsheviks
Russian Social Democratic Party 9
Russians
as ethnic group 89–90, 92
as political elite 93–4
dominance of 95
education opportunities 86–7

sex
and social inequalities 74–82
social change 5–6, 28–30
theories of 8
see also revolution
social class
and educational achievement 113–4
and higher education 108–12
and Marxist theory 4–33, 133, 135–7, 152
'New Class' 141–2
perception of 100
see also bourgeoisie; proletariat; social stratification
'social closure' 140–1
social inequality 31, 35, 52–3, 152
and consumption 62–6
and ethnicity 82–92
and income differentials 54–62
and influence of nuclear family 157
and sex 74–82
between industrial workers and farmers 40–2
between manual and non-manual workers 46–52